BeinG FranK

my time
with frank
zappa

Photos by Phil Stern • Illustrations by Suzy Beal

BeinG FranK

my time
with frank
zappa

nigey lennon

California CLASSICS BOOKS

LOS ANGELES, CALIFORNIA

Dedication and Acknowledgments

DEDICATION

To Bruce Cook, for believing in it, and to Frank V. Zappa (1940-1993), without whom...Something/anything, late as usual.

ACKNOWLEDGMENTS

To Steve ("Spud Man") Laufer, for use of his bathroom; to Ronald ("Dr. Mac") Van Ammers, for printing out all those copies of the manuscript; to Ken ("Mr. Photoshop") Boor, for taking 20 years off my life; to Suzy Beal, for coolness beyond the call of duty; to Lionel ("The Mac Butcher") Rolfe, for not getting upset despite fair cause; to Eric ("What's That Vegetable?") Weaver, for his total recall of the lyrics to "Billy the Mountain"; to Julia Stein, Victoria ("Women Who Swim with the Mud Sharks") Berding, and Ben Strout, for their editorial suggestions; to Phil Stern, for coming through as always, despite the vagaries of fame and fortune; and to Girlie, Wuzz, Bubba, JC, Buzz, Foon, Whitey, Loeb & Leopold, "Green" Ham, and The Professor, for making it impossible for me to work for very long.

Book design and typographical guru: Ken Boor, The L.A. Type

'Pataphysical layout suggestions: N.L.

Positivism: Aaron Silverman

Cover photo © 1995 Phil Stern
Author photo © 1995 Steve Laufer

California Classics Books
P.O. Box 29756, Los Angeles, CA 90029

Table of Contents

1940-1993

"We have to train ourselves so that we can improvise on anything — a bird, a sock, a flaming beaker! This, too, can be music. Anything can be music."

— *From Frank Zappa's film,* Uncle Meat, *1968*

The present-day composer refuses to die.

– Edgard Varèse

CHAPTER 1

Meet Mr. Honker

I n 1966, as an eleven-year-old eccentric in Manhattan Beach, California, I underwent a religious experience at the Unimart department store.

It was a lazy afternoon, and I had rather aimlessly hiked a mile or so uphill from my parents' house to the crossroads of the world — the corner of Sepulveda and Manhattan Beach boulevards. From the traffic signal at the northwest corner of the intersection I could see an endless stream of Ford Rancheros, metal-flake pickup trucks, Big Daddy Roth-customized surf wagons, and convertibles, all full of blonde people headed for the beach. I disliked the beach — not so much the sand and waves, but the rancid, oily smell of Coppertone and the horselaughs from the naugahyde-skinned adolescents who clogged the shoreline, boards in hand, praying for a tsunami.

The coolly-lit interior of the Unimart store was more anonymous, and for a few minutes, as I prowled the aisles, now fingering a set of brightly-colored acrylic yarn pot holders knitted in Taiwan, now crossing over to the hardware section and gingerly hefting a socket set that seemed to be made from cast iron, I could envision myself doing anything: living in a cottage in a Kansas cornfield, with frilly curtains at the windows, and salvaging scraps of the past to sew beautiful quilts from; or laboring long into the night to construct an immensely complex machine, a vast network of galleries and pulleys and billowing steam tow-

1

ering hundreds of stories high and requiring endless adjustments which only I could make. I imagined myself accepting the Nobel prize wearing greasy coveralls, wrench in hand, having just saved the world from imminent disaster by the turn of a single screw.

In the record department, The Troggs were whining "Wild Thing". Adenoidal Brits had become a *real problem* lately, clogging the airwaves with dreary, drippy exudations all too evocative of their dismal little island. I hated rock 'n' roll (although I kind of liked the ocarina solo in the break of "Wild Thing") — my personal hot pick at the moment was a 78, probably recorded some time during the 1920s, that I had scrounged from a pile of rejects at the Salvation Army. On the "B" side was a lilting waltz called "In Blossom Time" with a lovely contralto vocal by an entirely unknown singer, Mary West, and Full Orchestral Accompaniment by, I think, Harry Golden. On the "A" side, Harry and his orchestra performed without Mary, a hot jazz number which I only listened to once. It was on the *Conqueror* label, and listed on the wrinkly brown paper sleeve  were many other Conqueror discs, available for fifteen cents. I spent a great deal of time poring over the titles and artists and wishing I could still buy the records at places like Unimart. I liked everything about 78s — the big round labels with the exotic lettering, the thick weight of the shellac, the stylized vocals of the singers, the ticks and pops accenting the music, the way the needle raced like crazy across the wide, shiny grooves, finally running out of space and slapping furiously against the little ridge that separated the playing surface from the label. In sharp contrast to this *thrilling shellac universe*, rock music came on thin plastic 33 1/3 r.p.m. stereo discs with tiny grooves and dull, mass-produced-looking, non-hand-lettered labels — light in weight and in content. The whole idea of it bored me.

I drifted down the bins of albums, looking at the covers. There weren't all that many records; this was about five years before the *profitability level* of rock 'n' roll was discovered by multinational conglomerates. The paltry stock was segregated by plastic dividers with black block letters announcing TEEN FAVORITES, EASY LISTENING, DIXIELAND, GOSPEL...

In the TEEN FAVORITES ghetto I flipped through Bob Dylan's

"Highway 61 Revisited," the Rolling Stones' latest release, a couple of collected-hits packages, and altogether too much Sonny & Cher. Cher was no Mary West, and Sonny certainly no Harry Golden. (Tiny Tim and his ukulele weren't yet a cloud on the pop music horizon.) Suddenly I stopped cold. A black-and-fuchsia-and-blue album had literally and figuratively jumped out at me! I had never seen anything remotely like it in my life. From the cover glared the menacing faces of savages with long, matted hair and beads, the photo crudely colored over with what looked like a smeary crayola. They bore no resemblance whatsoever to the simpering, Prince Valiant-coifed rock groups on every other album cover — these guys looked like they'd steal your dog and eat it alive and kicking, if they got the chance. On the back cover was a typewritten note with a hand-printed signature by one Suzy Creamcheese, describing how these degenerates had been hired to play at her high school prom and had ruined it. The band was called The Mothers of Invention, and the album entitled "Freak Out!". Without knowing why, I felt I had to own it.

"Freak Out!" was a double album, two discs in a foldout cover, price $7.98. I checked inside my little green vinyl coin purse and found a quarter and a dime (I'd skipped lunch at school that day). Back home I had four dollars and some change stashed in a jewelry box, my life savings. I sighed and hiked back down the hill.

My mother was in the living room, watching "Dark Shadows" on TV and shortening a secondhand dress, turning it into a blouse. She made all her own clothes, not from patterns but by creating new things from old ones. At the time I thought this was extremely tacky and wished she would use patterns like anybody else. Later I would come to realize that the motivation for her idiosyncratic tailoring was a strange and complex convolution of childhood poverty (even though we were staunchly middle class and she could have afforded new clothes if she'd wanted them), her own inherent creativity, and a fierce defiance I never fully understood.

I told her there was a new record I wanted to buy, but that I was about a dollar and a half short. She looked up from the sewing machine with faint irritation. "You've got lots of records," was all she said, and went back to her work.

For the next two weeks I went without lunch. This wasn't much of a hardship — the food in the school cafeteria was famous up and down the state for being the worst in California, perhaps in the nation, at least in my humble opinion, and there was always the solace of cookies

3

or bread and cheese when I got home from school, to tide me over until dinnertime.

Finally, one Wednesday afternoon, I toiled back up the hill to Unimart and went straight to the record department. I paged through the selections in front of the TEEN FAVORITES divider until I got to the plastic card itself. Nothing. No "Freak Out!". Somebody richer had beat me to the punch.

I survived the disappointment somehow, and Unimart eventually restocked. The first time I played my very own copy of "Freak Out!", I didn't know quite what to think. The dog-killer image was certainly appropriate, but there was also a strong intellectual context. As for the music, it wasn't quite rock 'n' roll, or I wouldn't have listened to it more than once, but it definitely wasn't "In Blossom Time," either. There was too much shouting, mumbling, and fulminating, for one thing, not to mention a *lot* of percussion, and a xylophone on some of the songs. I was used to xylophones; I had a little three-octave student model, received one year as a Christmas present (I still don't know why), and on which I had been attempting to play the xylophone theme from "Danse Macabre" for at least three or four years. (I never could get past the place near the beginning, where the sixteenth notes started, without getting tangled up and dropping at least one of the mallets.)

Then there were endless liner notes in very small type on the inside of the album; I read them studiously, over and over, trying to understand what they meant. By the time I had them memorized, I was beginning to get a vague idea that "The Mothers of Invention" wasn't really a bunch of savages. "They" seemed to be extensions of one person, a fellow exotically named Frank Zappa (I wondered if it was a psychedelic *nom-de-guerre*). His presence permeated the entire record, but he was only visible in an underexposed photo on the left hand side of the inner spread as a very large nose, a striped pullover, and a hand holding a drumstick. A dialogue balloon issued from his invisible mouth: **"Freak Out!"** in Cooper Black, flopped so it read backwards. The note beside this image stated: "*Frank Zappa* is the leader and musical director of *THE MOTHERS of Invention*. His performances in person with the group are rare. His personality is so repellent that it's best he stay away...for the sake of impressionable young minds who might not be prepared to cope with him. When he does show up he performs on the guitar. Sometimes he sings. Sometimes he talks to the audience".... And the zinger, at the end: "Sometimes there is trouble." *Yeah!*

There was an additional bunch of quotes from whom, in my inno-

4

cence, I assumed to be very important people (although I'd never heard of a single one of them), warning how dangerous and crazy this Zappa character and his semi-musical concept were. Zappa had also listed his own influences: "These People Have Contributed in Many Ways to Make Our Music What it is. Please Do Not Hold it Against them." Among the culprits were Charles Ives, Lawrence Ferlinghetti, Pierre Boulez, Karlheinz Stockhausen, Anton Webern, Igor Stravinsky, Edgard Varèse, Maurice Ravel, Eberhard Kronhausen, Ravi Shankar, and dozens of blues and R&B musicians. I was too young to get the in-jokes, but I recognized some of the classical composers.

I played the two discs endlessly, trying to absorb the multitude of musical styles and attitudes. This was nearly two years before "Sgt. Pepper's Lonely Hearts Club Band" "introduced" the *Concept Album* to surf music-benumbed American teens, and even though I was used to extracting all the information from recordings, from the data on the label to the graphic design to the details of the music itself, "Freak Out!" was far over my eleven-year-old head. All I knew was that it sounded entirely different from anything I had ever heard before, and that it was hypnotically engrossing. Somehow I couldn't help playing it over and over and over.

"Freak Out!" was Frank Zappa's first album. I had no idea of its genesis, or that Zappa had been steadily crawling upward from the socio-musical garbage dump of Antelope Valley rhythm & blues bands and Inland Empire lounge shows, working truly horrifying day jobs and scoring no-budget movies, until he finally got his big break. I wasn't old enough to understand that "Freak Out!"'s target audience was the groovy Sunset Strip crowd, guys in tight white Levi's and girls with flowing blonde hair, both sexes coolly regarding the world from behind Ray-Ban sunglasses. None of it had very much to do with me, and yet as I listened to songs like "You're Probably Wondering Why I'm Here," I could imagine the surfing culture around me, and draw my own conclusions.

A few weeks after buying "Freak Out!", I found myself sitting with my acoustic guitar, trying to work out chords I could hear plainly in my head but lacked the knowledge and technique to wring from the instrument. It was frustrating, but I could feel that something was changing in the way I thought about music. Plain old open G sounded really stupid all of a sudden; I desperately needed *a whole new musical vocabulary*.

I went to the Gene Lees Guitar Studio on Sepulveda, and after hovering nervously near the sheet music for nearly an hour, finally got up the nerve to ask a clerk for a "good guitar chord book." The kid was one of seven Catholic boys from an otherwise upright family; he and his brothers all played in various local bands and rarely spoke to mere mortals. Without looking at me, he gestured vaguely in the direction of the Mel Bay and Mickey Baker folios in a distant corner, meanwhile continuing to mutter seductively to his girlfriend on the telephone. Mortified, I shuffled over and fumbled through the merchandise. The cheapest thing was a Guitar Chord Finder, printed on a clear plastic wheel that turned to transpose various voicings into different keys. It went into the pick compartment of my guitar case, where it remained, unmolested, until I finally sold the guitar a few years later so I could buy my first electric guitar.

But stumbling onto "Freak Out!" marked the end of my childhood, musical and otherwise. Although I never lost my fondness for lilting waltzes or slow drags, or any of the other pleasures of *hard-core shellac*, I developed into a rabid Frank Zappa fan. After several years and a few more Mothers of Invention albums, I began to understand the in-jokes, and I started buying albums of music by some of the composers Zappa had listed on "Freak Out!" — Stravinsky, Varèse, Webern. He turned out to be right: it *was* interesting music, much more interesting than rock 'n' roll.

Around this time, I wandered into the band room at school one day and there I saw, unwatched, a timpani, a gong, and some orchestra bells. I'd been taking piano lessons off and on for a couple of years, and I had my little xylophone at home, but in the back of my mind was this lurking question: What was it like to **bang on something *really loud***? Well, I answered that question in short order. My research was so thorough and so satisfying that South Bay Unified sent my parents a bill for the damage. After popping my percussion cherry, as it were, I began to regard George Antheil and Harry Partch as sex gods. I even had a moody-looking mezzotint of Quasimodo taped to the inside of my locker.

My songwriting, meanwhile, rapidly metamorphosed into a long catalogue of psychotic ditties which, if my parents had ever heard me perform them, would undoubtedly have landed me in some behavioral psychologist's bunker. None of the *boys* I went to school with were capable of writing such demented songs — much less the girls, most of whom had long stringy hair and liked to sit around under trees at lunch period looking soulful and warbling "Blowin' in the Wind" to out-of-tune nylon-string guitars. There was something "blowin' in the wind" in my case, all right, but it sure didn't *smell like teen spirit*. If I could have grown a mustache or tattooed a scale model of my menacing hero on my chest, just for the shock value, you bet I would have.

My troubles escalated when I entered high school. I should probably explain that during this time the South Bay, where I lived, had a sizable Catholic population, and those families who couldn't afford parochial school sent their kids to the "gentile" public schools. I used to refer to Mira Costa High School, my alma mater, as "Our Lady of Guacamole." Since nearly everybody who was on the South Bay Unified school board in the 1960s has gone on to *better things*, I can at last reveal the truth about the December Plot of 1969.

It had been the custom in Manhattan Beach, ever since the time of Columbus no doubt, to install a nativity scene on the front lawn of City Hall during the Christmas season. This holiday device consisted of a plywood edifice with a fake thatched roof, beneath which papier-mache statues of Joseph and Mary and the Three Wise Men flanked a particle-board manger containing a bundle of rags that was supposed to represent the newborn Baby JC.

On Christmas morning, 1969, the townspeople of Manhattan Beach awoke to find that a few *shifts* had been made in the *paradigm*: in place of the manger, there was an American Standard toilet on which was enthroned a life-size, naked dummy of Frank Zappa with his pants down around his ankles. (This was at a time when every frat house in the country had at least one copy of Zappa's notorious "Phi Zappa Krappa" poster prominently displayed.) The blasphemy, when discovered, was hastily whisked away, although the manger couldn't be found, which left a gaping hole between Mary and Joseph and made some wags ask, "Is He risen?" (*meaning Zappa from the throne*). The culprit was never publicly determined, but the folks at American Martyrs Church would have added *me* to their list of sainted sufferers if they had gone around to the back of my boyfriend's garage, where the purloined holy fodder-trough had been gleefully dismantled and stashed.

That year I was a sophomore at Our Lady of Guacamole, and in and out of several bands when I wasn't in detention or explaining my latest misdeed to Miss Rissé, the girls' vice principal. Other people who were in high school during the late 1960s may have been merrily trafficking in sex, drugs, and rock 'n' roll, but at *my* high school all the history teachers were John Birchers and the really cool thing to do after school was paint curbs for De Molay. Weekend surf gremmies were considered wickedly avant-garde. *Why me, Lord??*

To compensate for my misery, I had moved on to electric guitar, and still under the Zappa influence, I was composing dismally ambitious works with titles like "Adolf Hitler's Bunker and the Young Porsche" and "The Sun City Fertility Rites." (One of my fellow musical miscreants was another Our Lady of Guacamole student, David Benoit, a descendant of William Jennings Bryan. Dave, who suffered from dermatitis, played piano in several of my anarcho-musical outfits, but he fortunately somehow survived my bad influence and went on to considerable financial glory in the twilight musical world where Henry Mancini meets Bill Evans and scores a total K.O.) I was also the first chair percussionist in the South Bay youth orchestra, where I spent my time snoring through Haydn and languishing for an opportunity to whomp the dust off my mallets with some Stravinsky or Bartok. (I was relieved of this position after launching into a very loud jazz shuffle rhythm on the adjacent timpani during an otherwise quiet stretch in the annual Handel "Messiah" extravaganza.)

During summer vacation my boyfriend and I began recording some of my songs on my father's Viking stereo reel-to-reel tape deck. I played guitar, percussion (including an incredible four-octave toy piano I had found thrown out on trash collection day — both its black and its white keys were functional, and when operated with both hands it sounded like a cymbalom recorded on a wire recorder and played back too fast), a cheap little electric chord organ I had bought at Woolworth's, and ocarina (maybe that ocarina solo on "Wild Thing"*had* left a subconscious residue). My boyfriend played cello, harmonica, and jew's-harp, and we both sang. The songs included a ditty inspired by a visit to the La Brea Tar Pits, "The Bones Go Down (The Tar Pits Need Deodorant)," sort of a deconstructed "Them Bones Them Bones Them Dry Bones," and a mutant jug band number, "Moonlight on the Iceplant."

By now Frank Zappa, still my musical idol, had dissolved his old band, the Mothers, and had released "Hot Rats," a mostly instrumental album and my absolute favorite so far. How many gloomy, ocean-sticky nights had been illuminated for me as I dragged the phonograph tone arm back over and over, hogging out the near-the-end groove in "It Must Be a Camel" where the guitar, the sax, and the electric violin all played that incredible melody over those amazing chords during the final restatement of the theme? I'd gone through three copies of the album trying to dope out the voicings. Zappa was also producing albums by other musicians, most notably Captain Beefheart's "Trout Mask Replica," which, after Zappa's music, was the most interesting record I'd ever heard. I noticed in the fine print that both "Hot Rats" and "Trout Mask Replica" were released through Bizarre/Straight Records — the address was in Los Angeles. I began daydreaming about being produced by Zappa. It seemed logical enough to me: everybody said I was weird, so I was probably some sort of genius. If anyone in the music world could appreciate my unique talents, it would have to be Frank Zappa.

Right before school started, when my boyfriend had left for a vacation in Oregon with his family, I carefully wrapped up the reel of tape (there was only one; I never thought of making a dub rather than entrusting my lone copy to the Fates), wrote a brief note to Zappa explaining what the tape was, along with my address and phone number, and crammed everything into a big envelope, which I mailed off to him.

I figured I'd hear from him within a week. I stopped going anywhere I absolutely didn't have to go, so I could keep tabs on the phone and the mail. A week went by — no word; then another, and another. School began again, and I had to abandon my vigil by the phone. Our mailman regained his former geniality. But I hadn't lost faith; I knew I'd be hearing from Zappa. He was, after all, a busy guy.

In the end, it was nearly four months before the afternoon when I came home from school and found a lime green envelope, addressed to me, on the dining table. The minute I recognized the Bizarre Records logo, with its broken, angular letters, my heart began to pound. I sank into a chair, ripped open the envelope, and pulled out the sheet of lime green paper inside. It was only a few typewritten lines:

January 6, 1970.

Dear Nigey:
I am sorry not to have responded sooner. I am about to leave for a European tour but would like to discuss your tape when I return.

Sincerely,

Frank Zappa

The written signature looked like a sexually deviant strand of linguine.

I carefully returned the letter to its envelope and put them both in my school notebook. The next day I pulled the note out and read it so many times that it started to look like dirty money from Tangier. I showed it to a select group of people, mostly other musicians at school who had been known to sneer at me before because I was so weird. I'm sorry to say that I instantly ascended to the topmost pinnacle of that segment of school society, solely on account of the cheap celebrity generated by my receiving a letter from Frank Zappa. Evidently my weirdness wasn't so weird after all, if the chief weirdo of all time had expressed an interested in my music.

But as the month crept by, my apprehension began to mount. What exactly was I going to say to Zappa when I saw him? It was one thing to fantasize about being produced by my musical idol, but I had no idea, beyond whatever impressions I could gather from his records, what he was actually like. I had yet to attend one of his concerts; I'd just started to learn to drive. I hadn't mentioned my age in my letter. Maybe he'd laugh me out of the office when he saw that I hadn't even turned sixteen.

Around the time I thought Zappa would probably be back from Europe, I called Bizarre Records at the phone number on the letter. Trying to sound mature and somewhat supercilious, I asked the woman who answered if I could speak to Mr. Zappa. She had a cultured British accent and was admirably evasive, so I tried reading her the letter. It was obvious that she thought I was making it all up, but I did manage to get her to take my name and number; Mr. Zappa was due to stop by the office at the end of next week, she said distantly.

The next afternoon the phone was ringing as I came through the door after school. I got to it around the eleventh ring, and much to my amazement there was the cultured British accent. She said that Mr. Zappa had received my message and wanted to know if next Wednesday at 3:30 p.m. would be acceptable. Here was an immediate obstacle: my last period at school didn't end until 2:30, and the address on the letter said that Bizarre Records was located on Wilshire Boulevard. To get from Manhattan Beach to the Miracle Mile in an hour was possible, but not on the bus. I hadn't yet obtained my driver's license. In those innocent days suburban teenagers didn't routinely cut class or drive without a license, and neither could I.

I quickly said that 3:30 p.m. would be fine, and asked for the cross street, since I had only been on the Miracle Mile a few times in my life (one of those times being the trip to the La Brea Tar Pits). Then I ambushed my father when he came home from work and proceeded to bludgeon him with histrionics. If he didn't give me a ride next Wednesday afternoon, I assured him, I'd never have a music career and I'd be a total stumblebum and disgrace him in his old age. (At least I've made one or two accurate predictions in my time.) He grumbled considerably, but it was worth it. At 2:33 p.m. the following Wednesday, my boyfriend and I jumped into my dad's *I'm-over-40-to-hell-with-it-I'm-getting-a-muscle-car* Buick Riviera in the Our Lady of Guacamole parking lot, and at 3:21 we were in the elevator of the nondescript skyscraper where Bizarre Records had its offices.

The woman with the British accent turned out to have flaming red hair and was wearing a plum-colored paisley velvet mini-dress. I thought she gave me an arch look as she indicated an overstuffed, tapestry-covered sofa in the reception area, but I was too busy being terri-

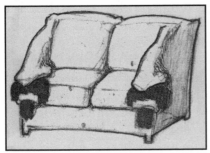

fied to care. I had dressed in my hippest clothes — cowboy boots, tight jeans, a gold silk shirt with flowing sleeves, and a paisley scarf tied elaborately around the neck of the shirt. While we waited for Zappa, I tried to calm myself by studying the framed concert posters on the wallpapered walls, but it was no use.

I could barely stay on the sofa. I lit a cigarette, but when I nearly set my sleeve on fire I hastily snuffed it out and stuffed it, minus two puffs, into an ashtray.

Fortunately I didn't have to suffer long: it probably wasn't a minute past 3:30 when Frank Zappa strode through the door, greeted Miss Accent, told her to hold his calls, and raised an eyebrow at us. "Hiya," he said. He had my tape box under his arm. I don't think I ever felt so important in my life — or so fraudulent.

We traipsed behind him down a short hall into an office, and he shut the door behind us. He brushed against me lightly as I awkwardly turned to sit down, and I looked up at him. He was 29, fourteen years my senior, and he had a stylized face, like an actor playing a medieval Venetian nobleman in a European silent film: square jaw, sharp nose, black mustache and Imperial goatee, thick, squiggly ink-black curls pulled back in a ponytail. His eyes were the most startling thing about him — large, deep-set burnt-sienna pools, dark-circled, externally and internally reflective. The usual social boundaries didn't seem to exist for him; when he looked straight into me with those laser eyes, there was no doubt that he was attempting to make a direct connection.

His manner towards us was reassuring, though — jovial and kindly in a droll sort of way. He seemed to relish playing the comic role of a somewhat demented philosopher-king attempting to explain the facts of life and art to a couple of raw young disciples. The monarch even had a crown — I couldn't help but notice that he was wearing a green-feathered lady's hat. ("Junk store item," he explained, when I remarked on it.) On any other six-foot male with his appearance, that hat would have seemed aberrant, but it lent Zappa a cartoonishly jaunty air that fit him perfectly.

a very odd hat

Looking at him sitting there regarding us solemnly, but with a strange humor, I had an ill-defined, unsettling feeling about him, the sense that although he was quite approachable, he was also rather distant. No matter how long someone might know him, there was no way they could really get into his mind.

Meanwhile, there he was, patiently waiting for me to speak up and say something coherent, and I couldn't squeeze out a single word. I was too mesmerized by his proboscis. **What a honker!** It was narrow at the bridge, but its downslope was so precipitous that it really seemed to defy gravity. Coupled with those glowing, laser-beam eyes, it gave him the look of a hawk that had gone without dinner one night too often.

Frank couldn't help noticing that I was gaping like an idiot. He inquired elaborately, "Something the matter?" I managed to stammer out a few inco-

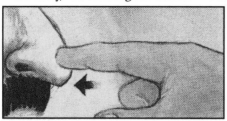

herent syllables to the effect that I found his nose fascinating.

Whereupon he leaned across the desk toward me and *stuck the organ in question right in my face. "Wanna feel it?"* I reached out a rather unsteady hand and gave it a feeble tweak. "You OK now?" he asked afterward. I giggled and nodded.

With this weighty matter duly resolved, Zappa reached into the pocket of his brown tweed blazer and pulled out a piece of paper on which there were copious notes in fine, crabbed script — the deviant linguine again. Then he launched into the first couple of lines of "The Bones Go Down"! I was totally disarmed; between the nose-fondling ritual and now actually hearing him sing *my* lyrics, he could have knocked me over with his hat.

He regarded me gravely for a moment, waiting until I regained some semblance of composure. When I didn't, he cleared his throat and began, "My father said that the road to hell was paved with good intentions." He gave me a knowing look and continued, "I like some of these songs..."

"Do you want to produce them?" I blurted out. Zappa shook his head. "They're not ready to record yet," he replied. "You're still just farting around; you need to get *serious* about what you're doing." He spoke precisely and and a little dryly, with ironic emphasis on certain words that made his comments seem extremely humorous or else somewhat threatening, if you happened not to have a sense of humor.

I felt very confused. I was having trouble concentrating — there was something about his voice that seemed to be tickling me in embarrassing places. I glanced up. He was looking right at me, and his eyes were gentle, droll, and more than a little affectionate. How did he know?

He wanted to know who had played the guitar on the tape. I told him I had. "In a few more years you might be a good guitarist," he said, "but you need to practice your scales and arpeggios. You're trying to play too fast; what you need to do is slow down and think about what you're playing. It's better to play a few notes that express something honest than a whole cloud of gnat-notes that don't say anything." He was right again — I did tend to play way too fast, hoping nobody would notice anything but my apparent virtuosity.

Zappa had listened carefully to the tape, and he made comments on all the songs. His perceptions were uncannily accurate; in fact, it struck me that his sizing-up of my entire state of mind bordered on the psychic, maybe even the psychotic. Of course I was only fifteen, and trans-parent, and he had, after all, made it his business to keep in touch with the mental aberrations of his adolescent fans, but his avuncular commentary hit so close to home that it was frightening me. I argued with him a little about his assessment of the material, and he responded, "I think you're confusing your need to express yourself with your need to be accepted." Then he gave a side-

ways glance at my boyfriend and opined, "You're basically just horny — you need someone to love you."

I was speechless. I fancied myself complex and inscrutable, and he'd only just met me — so how could he be so sure I was sexually frustrated? But despite my internal splutterings, I knew he was right *again* (jeez, didn't he get tired of being right all the fucking time??). I hadn't really thought about it consciously before, but I *was* attracted to him. Maybe it wasn't quite the same thing as falling for the school football hero or some bleached-blonde ho-dad, but I'd been listening to his voice on those Mothers of Invention albums, and staring at his mug on the album covers, since pre-adolescence. *Programming* ... He was used to that, I figured. In fact, around the time I discovered "Freak Out!" I'd stumbled onto a tongue-in-cheek interview he'd done for a teenage fanzine in which he described his Dream Girl as "...an attractive pariah, with an IQ well over 228...no interest whatsoever in any way in sports, sunshine, deodorant, lipstick, chewing gum, carbon tetrachloride, television, ice cream...none of that stuff! In short — a wholesome young underground morsel open to suggestion!...PS. I might even like her better if she can play Stockhausen on the piano...*Klavierstucke XII...*." With his peculiar brand of self- confidence, he probably attracted lots of *suggestible morsels*. No doubt he stood back with that slightly predatory, ironic expression and let them fall all over him.

Frank put his feet up on the desk and moved on to other subjects. He asked us where we lived, what did we do every day, what kind of music did we listen to. I didn't want to come out and admit that I was in high school, so I beat around the bush and said I was "between situations." I doubt whether I fooled him, but he didn't let on that I hadn't.

We talked about our respective record collections, and he said quite humbly that he had "a fair-sized R&B collection" dating back to his high school days, which he still took great pleasure in listening to. I asked him what it included, and he rattled off a list of names: Guitar Slim, Clarence "Gatemouth" Brown, T-Bone Walker, Elmore James, Johnny "Guitar" Watson. The way he pronounced them just *radiated ecstasy*. He also regaled us with stories about his recent European tour. He'd gone there with Captain Beefheart, acting in the capacity of road manager. The low point of the tour, he explained, had come at a three-day festival in Amougis, Belgium, where both the gig and the sleeping accommodations were in a huge circus tent in a turnip field. Temperatures dropped down around freezing at night, and since Amougis was far from civilization, the only sustenance was in the form of frozen Belgian waffles and moldy wieners. "They kept those weenies in this big tank full of water, and you could see that the tips of 'em sticking out of the water were *green*."

I had never had such a good time talking to anyone before. Zappa was a marvelous storyteller, but he was also a good listener. When I or my boyfriend said something, he listened gravely, as if what we had to say was important. He never mentioned himself or his work unless we asked him a specific question — he seemed to prefer listening to us talk about ourselves.

It came as a shock and a letdown when he finally looked out of the window — the towering neon Mutual of Omaha sign was just blinking on behind him like an ornament on top of his green feathered hat — and, clearing his throat, gently let us know that he had other things to get to. More than two hours had passed in what seemed like ten minutes. As we stood up he gave me one last steady look and said, "When your stuff is ready, you'll be able to sell it anywhere, not just here." Seeing my glum expression, he added quickly, "But I'd like to hear it again when it's finished." He gravely picked up my tape box from the desk and handed it back to me. Then he reached down with his thumb and forefinger and gently twiddled the tip of my nose, where it turned up. Now his eyes were twinkling with wry affection. In a flustered blur, I stretched a couple of inches and kissed him on the cheek.

As I descended to the lobby in the elevator, it seemed as if every floor down was one step closer to mundane 'reality' — whatever *that* was. I felt as if I'd been struck broadside by an entire galaxy hurtling directly at me. Certainly nothing on the Miracle Mile was as intense and vivid as Frank Zappa and his strange universe in which we had been immersed for two hours, or maybe two million light years.

I had every intention of going back to work on the tape and resubmitting it to Zappa. I also restrung my guitar, bought some advanced chord and arpeggio studies, and vowed to spend every waking hour learning to play "honestly", if I could figure out what that was. But before I had a chance to start putting off all this work, other things intervened. The sporadic troubles I had always had with the authorities at Our Lady of Guacamole became chronic, then acute.

The campus dress code was rigid — when they made you kneel on the ground, the hem of your skirt had to reach all the way to the blacktop, or you were sent home to change into "more appropriate attire". Evidently the chiefly Catholic administration was convinced that miniskirts were the Devil's workshop. I thought the whole concept was absurd, and after ransacking the Goodwill store for a 1950s-vintage Catholic-schoolgirl plaid pleated skirt, I wore it to school with a pair of lug-soled Cub Scout hiking boots outgrown by my boyfriend's younger brother. For a blouse, I hunted up an old army-surplus fatigue shirt and stenciled my student ID number over the pocket. Result: *American Icon Hash*. At first I thought, much to my disappointment, that this attire was attracting no particular notice from the authorities. I hastened to add my boyfriend's Oshkosh B'Gosh overalls underneath the skirt, just in case my fashion statement was too subtle. That very day, as I was serenely puffing on a Camel non-filter behind the girls' gym, Miss Rissé happened to stalk by on a patrol. Like Anton Webern, who was shot to death by American Occupation soldiers when he went out on his porch after curfew one night to sneak a smoke, my career also ended brutally. I was duly apprehended and marched to the principal's office, where my father was called at work and I was summarily executed. And this wasn't Occupied Austria at the end of World War II, but Manhattan Beach, California in the good old USA, A.D. 1970. Imagine!

My parents obviously felt furious, cheated, and more than a little embarrassed that I'd been permanently excused from *learning to be a valuable member of society*, but they didn't say anything. No mention was made of my going on to continuation school, junior college, or any other institution. I had always imagined I would be a musician or at least a songwriter. Now it looked like I might have to settle for being a dishwasher — if I was lucky.

Then my grandmother, with whom I was very close, became ill, and I took the family's Dodge van (which had been bought on a whim in case my mother ever repented and allowed us to go on a camping trip) and went to Arizona to be with her in her last days. In the process I became involved first in riding and then in rodeo, and I put the idea of a music career on the back burner, although I continued to write songs whenever I was sitting in the van on a balmy, star-filled night with a fracture or a contusion. I still listened to Zappa's music as much as ever, too, and I sometimes thought about the things he had said during our meeting, and the way he had said them. I had begun to read books on Zen and Taoism, and I was trying to live in the moment as much as I could, but I suspected that somehow, in the inexplicable chaos of the universe, I'd run into Frank Zappa again.

16

CHAPTER 2

The Short Hello

C oming back to Los Angeles from Arizona was a *decompression experience*. My grandmother had died, and I felt as if a big chunk of the past was gone. I was a few months shy of my 17th birthday, and all I wanted to do was hide in a small mahogany-paneled and velvet-wallpapered room, draw the velvet drapes over the bay window, and listen to Blue Amberol cylinders on an Edison reproducer. Probably I should have gone to San Francisco. Instead, lacking any wherewithal whatsoever, I sheepishly checked back in at the Parental Hotel in good old quotidian Manhattan Beach. I had some vague notion of trying to study musicology or medicine; my mother felt that I should get a job and contribute to my upkeep.

This wasn't a half bad idea, but after three weeks of toting a 30-pound sack of junk mail and rubber-banding circulars onto doorknobs in Watts and Willowbrook, I was relieved when a position opened up in the shipping department of my father's furniture company. My dad had definite opinions about nepotism: His brothers were partners in the business, and their no-good kids had been given roomfuls of furniture by their doting fathers, for free. He expressed some concern about my reliability as an employee, but in the end he agreed to hire me on for $85 a week — fifteen of which I was to pay at home for room and board.

The situation turned out to be less than ideal. During my brief rodeo stint I had been knocked over and then kicked by a horse while team roping, causing fractures on several of the ribs nearest my lungs. Even now, more than a year later, I could feel it when I took a deep breath. In the process of schlepping bulky boxes across several hundred feet of slick concrete floor to the shipping dock and then loading them onto waiting trucks, I started to get pretty tired of gasping for air all the time. I didn't mind doing a man's work, but at five-eight and 130 pounds, I was built more like an intellectual than a stevedore. It was time for me to get back to more cerebral pursuits before I killed myself.

One day I was perusing the Los Angeles Times and noticed that Frank Zappa and the reconstituted Mothers (the "of Invention" had been quietly dropped when Frank started his own record label) were appearing locally. I had written a couple of record reviews for a local magazine, Coast, and I managed to schnorr a comp ticket to the show. I thought it would be entertaining to see Zappa again and find out if he remembered me after more than a year. The concert was a blast. I privately felt that the musicianship wasn't up to the standards of "Hot Rats" or some of Zappa's efforts with the original Mothers, but the material, as always, was interesting and highly varied — something to offend everyone.

After the show ended, I made my way to the backstage entrance. A meaty specimen in a rent-a-cop uniform thrust up an arm as big as a Virginia ham and blocked my access. "Sorry, dear, you have to have a pass," he simpered.

I feigned annoyed incredulity. "I just went out in the auditorium to watch the show," I explained testily. I heard a set of immense, rusty gears give an agonizing jerk and then painfully grind into action somewhere far back in his cranium. Before they could rotate very far, Zappa himself appeared, guitar case in hand. He spotted me and instantly acknowledged me with a *"Hey,"* raising one black eyebrow and his empty hand simultaneously. I fell in step beside him and was drawn along in his wake to the dressing rooms, leaving the rent-a-cop to find some Rustoleum.

"So what's up?" he asked, leaning his guitar case against a chair and putting his foot, in a snazzy caramel-colored Italian oxford, up beside it. He was wearing a blue knit polo shirt with a pattern of ombre stars. Reaching into its skin-tight pocket, he drew out a pack of Winstons, selected one, then offered the pack to me. I'd smoked a couple of cigarettes, chiefly out of nervousness, during our interview at Bizarre Records, and he remembered that fact. *Nice memory!*

"Nothing's up," I grinned, turning down the proffered smoke. "I enjoyed the show."

"Thank you veddy much," he said mock-courteously, then turned and began to attend to business, stuffing a sheaf of music paper into a big, serious-looking briefcase and snapping it shut. I could see that his eyes had a devilish gleam in them even though his mouth was poker-straight between his thick mustache and manicured goatee.

"Do you still have a band?" he asked, setting the briefcase beside his guitar and retrieving a white sheepskin coat that had been flung over a folding chair. "Not now," I replied. "I've been toiling in the family business — not much time for the good life, I'm afraid."

Zappa took a puff on his Winston and sat down on the table, facing me, his hawk like features wreathed in smoke. "We're doing a show in Berkeley in a couple of weeks," he said offhandedly. "If you came up there then, I'd be delighted."

"What do you have in mind?" Things around here were getting interesting *fast*. "How's your rhythm guitar playing?" he asked, side-stepping my question. "Fair-to-middling. I'm more of a lead player. Mostly what I've been playing recently is slide." "Blues?" His eyebrows bumped into each other across the bridge of his nose. "Western swing," I said. "I've been trying to get a lap steel sound in open tunings."

He grimaced. Evidently the Cowboy Way wasn't very high on his list. "Come up to the house next week and we'll run you through the stuff, see what you can do," he said, grinding out his cigarette on the floor. "Then we'll see."

"W-what's the address?" I asked, fumbling in my bag for paper and pen. My rooting around was fruitless; finally Zappa thrust a big black fountain pen at me, the type used to copy musical scores. I noisily scratched down the address he gave me, at the top of Laurel Canyon; how I'd get there was anybody's guess. I couldn't afford a car of my own on $70 a week.

"I've got to kick you out now," said Zappa matter-of-factly. "See you next week." He picked up his guitar, briefcase, and coat, then leaned over and kissed me lightly on the cheek. Somewhere down the cavernous hall I heard echoing voices and the sound of female laughter. Then without being able to remember how I got there, I was outside, behind the auditorium, blinking dumbly in the warm, late-summer night. Something was clenched in my hand. It was Zappa's Speedball.

Chez Zappa turned out to be a rambling, ranch-style split level at the apex of Laurel Canyon, near Mulholland Drive. I pulled the trusty Dodge van (wheedled out of my dad at the last minute, which saved me from having to hitchhike up Laurel Canyon Boulevard dragging my guitar case) into a wide driveway next to a new Mercedes sedan, hauled out my guitar, and walked up to what appeared to be the entrance gate, set in a tall wooden fence. I tried opening the gate; it wouldn't budge. "Hello?" I called tentatively, feeling intrusive. No answer. "Hello!" I reiterated. High above me the curtains parted in a tinted plate glass window. Then a female voice, a low alto, came crackling through a small speaker set in the fence to the left of the gate. "Push on the gate," it said. I did. There was an ominous electronic buzzing, and the gate clicked open to admit me, then slammed hard when I'd got through. *To the citadel...*

Looking ahead, I saw a sloping, freshly-mown lawn. A movie theater exit door stood open to the right. Suddenly a vivid and shocking guitar arpeggio burst through the door, ringing like a bell but piercing like a buzz saw. Hypnotized, I followed it through the doorway into an entirely purple room. It was like being *inside a purple explosion*: The walls, the ceiling, the doors were all painted the same deep and pleasing shade of heliotrope. In one corner was an eight-foot concert grand; in another, a tangle of blinking lights and tangled wires was joined umbilically to a four-track tape deck. A maroon Victorian sofa was piled with stacks of music and a tiny pair of child's saddle shoes. And in the center of it all sat Zappa, huddled in a big leather executive desk chair behind a Gibson Les Paul. He let loose another incredible chord and reached over and pulled his lit cigarette from the pegboard of the guitar where it had been stuck under the strings, billowing smoke like a grenade.

"Hey," he said, gesturing to an empty chair next to him. I sank into it, wondering why he was so terse with his greetings and farewells.

"I had a little trouble finding the place," I ventured as I opened my guitar case and took out my well-worn Gibson L5. Frank ignored this pleasantry and frowned at my guitar, a pre-World War II hollow-body with a De Armond pick-up. I had another, more modern instrument, a Gibson 335, but I had left it at home because the L5, my pride and joy, had such a full, warm tone.

"That's going to feed back like hell," he opined.

"No it's not. I've played it through lots of different amps. You can crank it pretty much all the way up."

"Not at the volume *we* play at. Here, you better use this." He handed me a little red Gibson SG, a *rock 'n' roll axe*. I gingerly touched the strings. They were the lightest gauge I'd ever seen, and the neck had been planed down until it was wafer-thin. The whole setup was completely alien to me; I was used to playing in a different era. Zappa, paying no attention to my discomfiture, unwound a guitar cord and gestured toward an amplifier. "Plug in over there. You want some coffee?" I nodded, and he reached for a tall thermos and poured a steaming stream of black brew more solid than liquid into a stoneware mug. No mention was made of milk or sugar. Reeking with bravado, I took a hearty slurp. Suddenly everything went black before my eyes, and I gasped. I silently blessed the old aluminum espresso maker that had lived on the back burner of my parents' stove, exuding gallons of granular, inky sludge for as long as I could remember. Today the fact that I'd been swilling 60-weight from infancy had saved me from a most ignominious end: *this stuff was industrial-grade.*

When I finally had my throat cleared, the guitar plugged in, and the volume adjusted, Frank whipped out the first chord chart. It swam under my eyes, a work of art copied precisely and delicately in calligraphy that was so clean it was almost prissy. While I was still peering at it, Frank picked up his guitar and counted off. Unprepared, I stumbled badly in the first bar, before he had a chance to begin his lead. "I-I don't think I know the fingering on this chord," I stammered, feeling my face flush.

Zappa didn't need to look at the chart. "That's A suspended fourth," he said. *Hmmm...* He demonstrated the fingering on his own guitar. "Try it again." We got a little farther along in the song, and then I tripped over another Walter Piston voicing. Frank enlightened me, and we went on. Actually, despite my screw-ups, I soon relaxed. I could feel that we had an intuitive mutual sense of rhythm and timing. Just as I had reveled in our first conversation, I rapidly lost myself in our musical dialogue. The chords and melody flowed effortlessly, and when I suddenly got carried away at one point and slipped into the lead, Frank shifted smoothly to rhythm. After letting me play through the head, he nudged me back into my accompanist's role by resuming with an extremely florid solo. His chord changes were considerably more complex and fluent than mine, but he made it plain that he had no desire to 'comp' behind anybody, least of all me. We ended the song together, neatly, and I looked up. My face felt like it was on fire. "*Whoo-ha!*" I exclaimed. "What a song!" Frank nodded, a slight smile visible beneath his mustache. "Make your eyebrows go up and down?" he asked. I chuckled at this picturesque figure of speech. "My foot too."

We worked our way through charts until my fingers were raw. After a couple of hours, Frank let me take a break. I was about ready to drop anyway. "Looks like you're working for Air, Moisture and Pain," he cracked, making a joke about my blistered digits and Blood, Sweat and Tears. He stuck out his left hand and showed me his own incipient calluses. "I ain't been so diligent myself lately 'bout practicing," he observed in a caricature of some raspy, mumbling blues singer. I found myself staring at his thumb the way I'd earlier ogled his schnozz. My hero was turning out to be a veritable prodigy of alien physiology, *The Beast With Ten Fingers*... His fingers were long and supple, but he had wonderfully flat, utilitarian thumbnails. *Why, he could have been a bricklayer and really made something of himself.* I was suddenly seized with an urge to stick his thumb in my mouth and suck on it. The impulse, which seemed to leap into my mind unbidden, made me blush, and I quickly looked down at the music in front of me; although he wasn't being crass about it, I suspected that if this were something other than a business-type situation, Frank would have been offering me any digit I happened to be interested in, and suggesting utilities for same.

When we resumed, I continued to have my share of trouble with unfamiliar chords, and a couple of times I could tell that Frank was a bit impatient with me. I didn't care, though. I had thought I liked his music before, when I was just a passive listener; but now that I'd actually gotten my hands on it, I felt like I'd received a reprieve from reality. It was as if I had slipped the dismal bonds of my mundane existence and emerged into a fiery realm where everything was exalted and not a little peculiar. By the time Frank finally called a halt to the runthrough, I was feverish, exhilarated, incoherent. I liked this new state of existence so much that the thought of leaving it was unbearable.

When we finally put down the guitars, Frank looked at me with an appraising expression. "Glad you enjoyed this little piece of the Project/Object," he said.

"The Project...?"

"The Big Note. Everything I do, and anyone involved in any part of it — it's all part of a larger composition. You could call it *conceptual continuity*." He said this with an immense gravity, as though he were explaining quantum mechanics, or the reproductive modalities of slime molds. But there was a glint of self parody in those resonant eyes; he obviously wasn't *entirely* serious.

Then Frank began to explain the situation with his road band. The group had been touring steadily during the past six months, and now, after a short break, they were about to embark on a very long U.S. and European tour with no time off at all. The main reason for this new tour was to promote Frank's newly-completed first feature film, *200 Motels*, and its soundtrack album. The tour would coincide with the opening of the movie in a number of test markets across the country, presumably reinforcing Frank's name recognition and expanding his consumer base. He handed me a very official looking press kit with the sort of marketing data, demographics studies, flow charts, and promotion strategies that are so dear to the hearts of executive types. I looked up from its bewildering mass of socioeconomic obscurantism, and there was Frank puffing away on a Winston, a veritable hipster Mephistopheles with his tangled mop of shoulder-length black curls, well-worn T-shirt, and faded Levi's with one of the fly buttons undone. Funny, he sure didn't *look* like a businessman.

The problem was, he went on, he was getting a *little bit concerned* about the mental and physical capacities of couple of the guys in the group. "Battle fatigue," he explained. "They're always on the verge of a Lost Weekend out there, and if they go mentally AWOL fifteen minutes before showtime, it can throw everything into total chaos." He put his index finger to his temple, indicating the mental state in question, and puffed on his cigarette, blowing out a little nebula of blue ectoplasm.

"Drugs?" I inquired.

Frank nodded but didn't elaborate. "It's not only the problem of selective amnesia brought on by recreational chemicals. We got a lot of dates on this tour with two shows a night. Laryngitis is always a lurking menace. Your assignment, should you choose to accept it" — he peered at me through his smoke cloud, with one eye half closed — "is to know all the material and be prepared to leap in at the first sign of an emergency, so that the people out there who come to see the show get their money's worth. Think you're up to it?"

He was asking me to be a ringer for the druggies in his band, huh? Sure, I could handle it. I felt a little like a detective in a pulp *noire* novel who, when faced with the classic impossible assignment, shrugs existentially and leaps into the unknown, possibly the fatal, without giving it a second thought. *Hell, baby, why not? I got nothing to lose.*

Before I could answer, there was a sound of footsteps and the creak of a door opening, and light flooded the dim top of the staircase that led down into the room. "Frank? You want some dinner?" In the background I could hear the small, crystalline voice of a child threatening to shatter into a tantrum. "You can bring your guest up too — there's plenty."

Frank stood up. For a microsecond he hesitated, then began to walk toward the exit door, away from the stairs. I picked up my guitar case and followed him. He stood framed in the doorway, waves of purple light behind him. "See you in Berkeley," he said, and closed the door between us.

I guess that meant I'd passed the audition.

The Unbearable Lightness of Berkeley

Things grew odder and odder as the day of my departure approached. A couple of nights before I was to join the tour, I was in the kitchen rinsing off the dinner dishes when I heard the phone ring in the living room, and my mother's voice: "Hello? Yes?" There was a pause, then, "You know, you ought to be ashamed of yourself, writing garbage like that..." By this time I'd figured out who it was and hightailed it into the living room to snatch the phone out of her hand before she could cause any more damage. My mother had been doing a slow burn for five years about this pervert's slimy influence over her only daughter; you couldn't blame her for seizing the day and giving him a piece of what passed as her mind.

When I tried to apologize, though, Frank just chuckled. It probably wasn't the first time he'd been attacked by outraged motherhood. "We seem to have a *demographic gap* here someplace," he intoned with pseudo-gravity, brushing aside my apology. He'd called to fill me in on some last-minute tour logistics. Needless to say, I did not embark on the tour with anything resembling my parents' blessings; if we'd had a cellar, they'd have clapped me in chains and locked me up in it.

Maybe they had a point. By the time I flew up to Berkeley for the show, I was in a trance, wandering around in a fractal cosmos made up of the atoms of an endlessly sustained eleventh chord. I had sneaked a surreptitious, very lo-fi recording of the recent L.A. concert on my portable cassette (Frank would probably have burned me at the stake if he'd known I'd done it; he seemed to feel it was grand larceny if somebody bootlegged a live show, even on a piece of junk like my $15 recorder. The first time he caught me making a tape of a show on the road, he seized hold of my little machine as if with the Hand of God, solemnly removed the tape, handed it back to me, and intoned, *"Turn this machine off, and may J never see you turn it on again while you're in this band."* I respected his wishes, and made sure he never saw me turn it on again — after that, whenever I used it I hid it under my jacket or somewhere else where it wasn't visible.) Luckily my tape was up to consistent pitch, more or less, and I'd been playing along with it, over and over, every day before leaving for the gig, so intent on it that I was stripped down to a raw, vibrating core.

As I staggered out of the Oakland terminal, I was downright dangerous. The objects around me — buildings, vehicles, billboards, even the grass and trees — had the aspect of a comic book illustration just on the verge of disintegrating around the edges. Back in those trippy times everybody in the universe under 30 was loading themself up with acid, hashish, peyote — but here I was, straight as a die yet swimming through a hallucinogenic universe at high noon. *When the mode of the music changes, the walls of the city shake,* said Plato, or Pliny the Elder, or one of those guys.

I found a cab and directed it to the edge of the Berkeley campus, where the auditorium for tonight's concert was located. It was 1 p.m.; the sound check was supposed to start at 2. Just as the cab was pulling up in front of the building, an enormous galvanized loading door in the back swung open, and a bobtail truck backed in beside it. Popular music, I reflected, was just like any other industry. The salable commodities had to be trucked across the country to the point of sale. It reminded me of working for my father. Oh well, whenever I got back from *this* little expedition, I probably wasn't going to have to worry about working for my father anymore.

I lingered across the street, watching, suddenly uneasy about barging right in. A sweet-faced young mother with blonde hair hanging to her waist walked near me, holding her toddler son by the hand. "Look, sweetie, look at the musicians," she said, pointing to the amplifier cabinets being hoisted up onto the loading platform. Everything seemed hyperrealistic and garish. I had no idea what to expect. *Anything could happen.*

When I couldn't stand to wait around any longer, I crossed the street and climbed up the steps that led into the auditorium. The equipment truck's back door came clanging down as I walked past. Inside, I nearly stumbled in the dark; sunlit trails still glared in front of my eyes. I could smell the warm dimness of an old auditorium, the moldering wool upholstery of the seats, the forgotten butts of a million and one cigarettes that had been hurled into the void for the past 75 years.

Some of the band members were already on the stage, tuning up. There was no sign of Frank. I was in the process of hesitantly introducing myself, meanwhile keeping a sharp lookout for the telltale signs of substance abuse, when all of a sudden I felt a pair of arms, surprisingly strong, grab me from behind. I turned around, and there he was: wild-haired, grinning like a buccaneer in the red light district, his eyes like exploding nebulae as he hugged me with mock ferocity. His mustache brushed teasingly against my cheek. "Heyyy!" he exclaimed. Then, feigning solemnity: "How do you like the *ever-so-spiritual Berkeley ambiance?*"

He had to do an interview before the sound check, and in his businesslike fashion he made sure I accompanied him when he went to sit down with the interviewer in seats several rows back in the auditorium. It was a technical discussion for Guitar Player magazine, and I listened carefully, hoping he'd reveal the true source of inspiration for his personal musical universe. He didn't, but if I'd been paying more attention to detail I could have undoubtedly duplicated his guitar style — he described it minutely, right down to his preferred string gauges, pickup configurations, amp EQ settings, favorite effects devices, the size and shape of pick he used, and a lengthy explanation of how he'd just discovered a perverse and thrilling "cream-puff effect" in the studio by pumping his guitar signal directly into the board. I wondered whether he was spouting techno-babble at least partly for effect; I'd never heard anyone sound so thoroughly immersed in the arcana of audio before. (By the time I left the tour two and a half months later, he had taken both of the pickups off my old Gibson 335, messed with the wiring, replaced them, fixed a longstanding string buzz, and changed the strings to a much lighter gauge — all in odd moments during sound checks or before shows. After he got done with 'my baby' I barely recognized it, so I let him keep it for the rest of the tour. But by then I understood that for him, 'tech' wasn't just a nifty way to get girls, it was his life's breath: *I putter, therefore I am.*)

After the interview, he got up, looked around for the errant band members, put two fingers in his mouth, and whistled shrilly. They all appeared from various nooks and crannies where they'd been stealing a hit or a snort, no doubt, and he herded them onto the stage like a football coach mustering the offense. Before I could ask him if I should join them, he had given the downbeat and kicked off a song. I sat down in the front row, feeling slightly crushed. They ran through the number, then Frank cut them off with a perfunctory but emphatic gesture. Evidently the sound was satisfactory. "See you back at the motel later," he told them, and jumped down off the stage.

He came over to where I was sitting. "Let's go," he said. At the exit we picked up a pleasant-faced fellow in his early 30s, I guessed (anyone over 30 seemed chronologically challenged to me — even, I'm sorry to say, Frank), who was standing around there as if he had nothing else to do. This was Dick Barber, the band's road manager, a down-to-earth sort of guy whose tonsorial style — balding on top, little ponytail in back — pre-dated by more than two decades the future Male Hollywood Showbiz Exec Look (minus the '90s regulation single earring).

The three of us walked out of the auditorium to a station wagon parked near the loading area. Dick climbed behind the wheel, I squeezed in next to him, and Frank rode on the outside; luckily the front seat was fairly wide, because two of us had *wider ones.*

We pulled out into the tree-lined Berkeley streets, dappled with light and shadow. In the distance the Oakland Bridge's massive gray exoskeleton, and the delicate rust-red spans of the San Francisco Bay Bridge, fluttered in the air like mirages. Farther off yet, the scrubbed white buildings on the San Francisco hills seemed to defy gravity, exploding into space from all directions, more light than matter. The breeze was cool, but I felt a thousand tiny flames licking my cheek.

I got up my nerve and asked Frank if I'd be playing with the band at the concert that night. He cleared his throat and shuffled his feet. "Most of it's going to be material you don't know," he answered. "I think it would be a good idea for you to listen to the show tonight and get an idea of the unfamiliar songs." That sounded reasonable enough. It was true — I didn't know a lot of the material. I hadn't had a chance to attend a full band rehearsal in L.A. before the tour started.

After a short drive down Shattuck Avenue during which I found myself staring intently at the billboards we were passing, the station wagon turned into the parking lot of the Berkeley House motel. I glanced sideways at Frank, who caught me looking at him. His eyes still had that mischief in them, although the playfulness had deepened into something a little more serious. Dick pulled up at the motel entrance, and fast as lightning Frank popped the door open and climbed out. I followed, with a sweaty feeling of anticipation.

We walked through glass doors into the lobby. There it was — that *unmistakable motel smell* of Lysol and naugahyde. The Muzak was pumping out a bassless, drumless, rhythmless rendition of "Light My Fire." We joined a gaggle of tourists waiting for the elevator. There were some sideways glances at Frank, a pronounced nervous drifting away from us as Mr. and Mrs. America sensed the menace lurking inside that brown tweed disguise.

Just then a couple of lads who looked like they were playing hooky from Cal came strolling down the hall on their way to the swimming pool. They spied Frank and immediately began gaping. The elevator, meanwhile, seemed to be hung up in the attic somewhere. Finally one of the boys summoned his courage: "Are — are you Frank Zappa?"

Frank nodded.

"Is it really true that you ate shit on stage?" asked the other guy with a nervous smirk. (This was a persistent canard that had been plaguing Frank at least since the late 1960s, but at the time I had never heard it before.)

Frank stared him down. *"That's a vicious rumor,"* he answered in his sardonic drawl. *"The closest thing to shit I ever ate was the Beef Wellington from the buffet at a Holiday Inn in Newark, New Jersey."*

The elevator door swung open just then, and as we piled in, we were confronted head on by the major disgust of Mr. and Mrs. America. Our middle-aged lady actually pressed herself flat against the side of the elevator as she entered, trying to avoid any possibility of contamination by this vile coprophage; her husband looked daggers at us from the other side of the elevator. Frank and I were suffused with smothered laughter, and by the time we were out of the elevator and into the upstairs hall, neither of us could hold it back. In front of the door to

29

room 303, we both collapsed, falling all over each other. I thought he was going to *die laughing*, right there in the hall of the third floor at the Berkeley House motel. Somebody get me a Steadi-Cam! **FRANK ZAPPA DIES LAUGHING!** *Film at 11!*

Finally Frank caught his breath and, snaking the room key on its plastic paddle out of his jacket pocket, he ceremoniously opened the door and gestured regally inside.

There were two queen size beds, both made up. A suitcase lay, open, across one of them. Frank flipped on the overhead light, then shuddered and flipped it back off. "A little moody lighting," he said, sitting down on the empty bed and switching the bedside lamp on low. Still in the doorway, I glanced around the room. The heavy curtains were drawn, letting in only the narrowest crack of light. Two dubious oil paintings of ships and lighthouses hung over the beds. A TV set stared out at us with its glass eye. There was music paper stacked neatly on top of the bureau beside the big black briefcase, a portable reel-to-reel tape recorder, and a pile of shrink-wrapped albums. A little leather shaving kit stood unzipped on the corner washstand, bulging with what I presumed was shampoo, razors, and whatnot. (I would soon have a *more accurate idea* of the nature of the paraphernalia in there.) On top of the neatly-folded things in the suitcase was a most unusual cap, a Martian extrapolation of yarmulke, porkpie hat, and jester's motley, with a star and a crescent moon suspended on top from a long fuzzy shank. The green-feathered monstrosity from our first meeting flashed ludicrously across my mind, and I found myself picturing Frank's *nice Italian Aunt Mary,* who must have gone in for surreal headgear during innocent little Frankie's most impressionable years, thereby turning him into a *millinery pervert* forever, before he even had a chance to know what was going on...

I turned my eyes around to Frank, still sitting on the bed, his shoes off but his socks on, calmly peeling off his orange "Jolly Gents" T-shirt. I wondered if he ever got tired out from his grueling schedule. Maybe he wanted to take a nap.

"Shut the door," he instructed me in a quiet voice.

I came in, closing the door behind me.

"You wanna come over here?" he asked nonchalantly, leaning back against the headboard. He was now attired in just his skintight Levi's and, evidently, no underwear.

30

The Unbearable Lightness of Berkeley

I looked at him, almost too overcome to do it but still compelled to. I had never felt so vulnerable, embarrassed, and confused before. The ironic, detached, yet somehow lubricious timbre of his voice, the way he looked up at me, seeming to understand everything and to be thoroughly amused about it, made me quiver all over. How could he know my feelings so much better than I did myself? I wished I knew what *he* was feeling, so I could figure out how to respond.

But as I stood there struggling with myself, I knew I had to own up to the real source of my discomfort. For me, Frank Zappa had gone from being a voice on the record player, a face on an album cover, an inspiring influence — to a very real, entirely corporeal 30-year-old guy who seemed to be about to casually seduce me in this crushingly ordinary motel room in Berkeley. I couldn't just put the disc into its jacket and stick it safely back on the shelf; I was being directly confronted by my hero, much larger than life and exuding a matter-of-fact sexuality that I found strangely embarrassing. Moreover, I could sense that it was this conflict of mine that was causing his own flame to flare up. If I'd simply been madly in love with him, he would probably have been bored to death. He needed to draw out and then conquer something in me; he must have relished the clash, or he wouldn't have created it in the first place.

I slowly walked over to the bed. I looked down at him, the crumpled pillows stuck behind his head, one arm tucked back under the pillows, all six feet of him radiating an attitude of sensual arrogance undercut by a marked awareness. He looked back at me coolly and levelly, both daring me and shrugging it off. Was he a human male, or an *idée fixe* ? I wanted to know him more than I'd ever wanted anything in my life, but I was terrified of what I might learn.

When I got down on the bed next to him, he put his arms around me, gravely, non-threateningly. Shaking all over, I plunged my face into the black hole that was his hair. It was so soft and thick I practically got lost in it. Before I could, Frank gently disengaged me, held me at arm's length, and gave me a searching look, not entirely without empathy or even sadness. "You sure you want to do this? I don't want to *coerce you against your will,*" he said, with exaggerated irony. I should have known he'd give me an argument. A peculiar combination of libertine and moralist, he wanted me to be aware of the consequences of this act; his tone of voice left no doubt that his intention was to be as thorough about

31

this as he was about everything he did, so I'd better be sure *that* was really what I wanted.

Still shaking, I nodded and tried to smile.

He reached across me and clicked off the light with a firm, decisive gesture. In the darkness of the room, the central air conditioning rattled the register in manic polyrhythms.

CHAPTER 4

Ride My Face to Seattle

lthough I didn't get to perform that night, I was on the stage for the entire show — sitting on a folding chair just a few feet from Frank but hidden from the audience by the tops of the amp cabinets. He was in an extremely jovial mood, ripping off brilliant solos and dancing around the stage like a maniac, conducting the band with such velocity I half expected his right arm to pop out of its socket. From time to time he'd shoot me a wicked look and throw a one-liner into the ongoing dialogue, a little in-joke that probably didn't carry any farther than my corner of the stage, but I was satisfied: I was a key proton in tonight's atom of the Big Note.

Needless to say, I wasn't paying a whole lot of attention to the material I should have been memorizing for the next show. I was vaguely aware of the structure of the songs and how they segued into one another, but usually about the time I 'd force myself to focus enough to make a mental note, Frank would raise the devilish old eyebrow at me. "Where can *I* go to get some Beef Wellington? Where can *I* go to get my *sock washed* ?" That one made me blush mightily, and Frank broke into a wicked grin. I noticed a couple of the guys in the band smirking at this byplay, and it suddenly hit me like a ton of bricks that *there is no such thing as private life when you're on tour with a band*. A valuable if somewhat disturbing realization.

When the show was over, the band piled into two station wagons for the trip back to the motel. Frank and I rode with Dick Barber again, this time letting him chauffeur while we sprawled out in the back seat; the rest of the band went in the other car, which had an additional seat in the cargo space and could accommodate everyone comfortably.

The good feeling from the concert hung over us in a pleasant haze, like decent brandy. Frank was leaning back against the seat with his shirt unbuttoned nearly all the way down, making little jokes and asides. The Northern California night had turned nippy, so I'd borrowed his old tweed blazer, which fit me surprisingly well. It was a *man's* jacket, with a nearly empty pack of cigarettes in one of the pockets and a (probably empty) lighter in the other; it exuded an elusive, musky scent of tobacco and leather. As I wondered idly why guys my own age didn't have interesting jackets like Frank's, he reached over, pulled me close to him, and put his arm around me.

I snuggled next to him, enjoying the feeling of quiet, steady warmth flowing out of him into me. I was a little surprised that being there with him was so relaxed and easy, and I found myself wishing the moment would go on forever.

Suddenly I heard Dick up front swearing, "*Shit...*" He had apparently made a wrong turn; we were headed away from University Avenue, toward the waterfront.

"Hey, Foon — think Simmons is hanging out there someplace?" said Frank, peering at the grim vista of ancient brick buildings and bleary streetlights. (Jeff Simmons, a former bass player in the band, had written a song called "Wino Man", alias "Wonderful Wino," about Skid Road in his hometown of Seattle. This tune had become part of the band mythology.)

Dick chuckled. Right then I felt the zipper on my jeans slide slowly and silently down, and an exploring hand steadily began to navigate its way around Cape Horn. "I think that's your right turn coming up," said Frank; from his tone of voice, he could have been reading the Christian Science Monitor. Nothing seemed to embarrass him.

By the time we finally got back to the motel I was limp, but Frank wasn't. We emerged from the car and passed through the lobby like a whirlwind. Fortunately the elevator was open and waiting. We emerged into the hall to find quite a little crowd gathered before the door of No. 303: assorted band members and other folks, including a highly miscel-

34

laneous collection of women. Everyone was in a rowdy mood, laughing and carrying on so loudly that I wondered why the motel management hadn't called the cops on us. It was already after one in the morning, but no one seemed to care. No wonder they called Berkeley "Berserkeley" in those days.

I glanced at Frank. He grinned. "Feel like doing some *entertaining*?" he asked. I didn't, but it wasn't *my* room. The party roared inside and piled onto the beds and chairs. There was considerable discussion of that night's show among the band members. The girls, exotic creatures dressed in fanciful costumes, laughed constantly, but said very little.

In the midst of the circus Frank, resting against the headboard of the unmade, windswept bed, maintained a genial but distant attitude. He should have been wearing a lab coat and making clinical notes on the proceedings. As a matter of fact, I would discover during the tour that he almost always had his portable tape recorder running, capturing conversations, situations, rehearsals, and scenes in motel rooms alike. He felt that anything that transpired on the road was part of the larger composition, so to speak, and just as valid as any other part of the composition. Some of the band members were inclined to regard this as snooping, stealing, or worse, especially when they subsequently found their own words handed back to them in the form of song lyrics or stage routines, but it didn't seem to bother Frank.

Frank seemed immersed in his observations, so I strolled down the hall to check out the scene in the room of one of the other guys in the band. The door was open and I found him sitting on the shag-carpeted floor sharing a sociable reefer with a dark-skinned, handsome girl wearing a patchwork velvet skirt and not much on top. They offered me a hit, but I smiled and politely explained that I didn't smoke dope. "You're kidding!" the girl exclaimed. "I don't know *anyone* who doesn't smoke. That's, like, the weirdest!" I was about to mention that Frank didn't, either, but the two of them had gone off into peals of hysterical laughter.

Just then the room phone rang. It was Frank, inquiring if I happened to be on the premises. I got on the phone and he made it plain that he thought I should be back in 303. When I hung up, the girl was looking at me with awe. "Are you with Zappa?" she asked incredulously. I nodded. "*Wow,*" she breathed reverently. On my way down the hall to Frank's room I mulled over the curious notoriety that seemed to be attached to being "with" a rock star. It didn't particularly bother me, but I did feel it was kind of cheap. After all, I was a musician in my own right — maybe not famous like Frank, but at least original. Wasn't *that* more impressive

35

than being "with" Zappa?

In 303, the party had evaporated. Frank was still propped up against the headboard of the bed; a statuesque brunette was perched on the edge of the mattress. I glanced warily at her — what sort of scene was this?

"This is Ramona," Frank said blandly. "She's a stripper, and she just mentioned that she's always had a fantasy about watching me, uh, receive oral gratification."

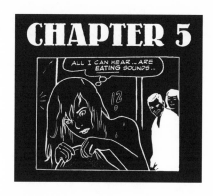

ALL I CAN HEAR ... ARE
EATING SOUNDS ...

CHAPTER 5

For *This* I Learned to Play Stravinsky???!

efore I was really aware of what was happening, it was too late: I had become inextricably involved with my guitar-wrangling boss. It wasn't as though he was on a campaign to convince me that he was Mr. Wonderful, but although I tried to keep a semblance of objectivity about the situation, there was just something addictive about being around him. Frank not only couldn't leave 'reality' alone, he was constantly *inspecting and customizing* it. In the afternoon of my third day on the road, as we were pulling into the parking lot of the motel prior to checking in, he was looking out of the car window at the landscape in his characteristic fashion, half intent, half relaxed, the ever-present cigarette in his hand. Suddenly he turned around and made a comment about how the place looked. I don't remember exactly the way he put it, but it was so succinct and at the same time so surreal and humorous that he sounded like the test tube offspring of Salvador Dali and some B-movie mad scientist. I had never before known anyone whose offhanded observations leaped right out of the confines of ordinary perception and into the fifth dimension like that. I had assumed that his anarchistic posturings and droll pronouncements were strictly theatrical, but now I realized that Frank's imagination didn't get packed away in a suitcase when he wasn't onstage or in the recording studio; *he thought that way all the time.* He was truly eccentric, much stranger and more interesting than I would have thought. I found myself wanting to inhabit his universe the way I needed to play his music.

It wasn't a one-way cosmos; Dr. Zurkon seemed to be delighted to have me around the lab. As a kid, he told me, his favorite form of recreation had been **blowing things up**, and he hadn't changed a bit in the intervening twenty or so years -- he'd just expanded his experiments into the human area. And here, suddenly, I was -- just in time to have my molecules thoroughly rearranged.

That afternoon, we had time to kill between the sound check and the gig. Once we had our suitcases stashed in our room, Frank, in a playful mood, asked me what I felt like doing. "Got a pair of trunks?" I inquired straightfacedly, looking out of the window at the chilly turquoise surface of the pool rippling in the stiff breeze two stories below.

"Nope," said my degenerate roommate with finality. To him, strolling from the car to the motel lobby was the equivalent of a back-pack expedition to the summit of Mt. Whitney.

Forced to invent other amusements, I flushed and mumbled, unable to specify what I had in mind, so the Grand Inquisitor commenced on me. Under his seemingly indifferent but actually concerted questioning, I finally confessed something that I'd first observed during our first encounter at Bizarre Records — the fact that I found the timbre of his voice almost painfully erot-ic. This seemed to delight him, and he immediately set about attempting, in his droll way, to *quantify my physical responses to his vocal apparatus. Clipboard. Pen. Lab coat.* Now, then: Did his voice by itself elicit an intense reaction? What if he changed the pitch? Well, how about changing the pitch and applying *this much* manual stimulation? OK, what happened when he *increased* the manual stimulation? Now let's introduce that *sock* I apparently was so fond of the other day...had it right there in the suitcase, hadn't rinsed it off yet, figured he'd need it again before too long. Vaseline? Nope, I was obviously a purist. So what happened when he *pressed his face against my solar plexus*? ...Hmm — would it *damage the beauty of this experience* if he asked me to attenuate the volume just a little, by any chance, say five or ten db? Security had their office on *this* floor.

I don't think Frank had anticipated how intensely I'd respond. I hadn't, either. I had been uncomfortable enough initially, but I rapidly became unbent: This mutant universe was becoming more exhilarating than I'd ever thought possible. Emotions were unrecognizable, thrills were much more intense because of their unfamiliarity, no longer did things resemble the monochromatic 'reality' I'd always taken for granted.

"Is there a word for 'love' in your universe?" I asked. By the time we left the motel for the show that night, I had an exciting new addition to my vocabulary — can you say *"polymorphous"* , boys and girls?

I began learning a few other things too. After a couple of days of engaging in *optional recreational activities* , as he called them, I realized that Frank's sexual philosophy was as original and as faintly disturbing as was everything else about him. He went after things that were important to him with a Zenlike absoluteness — and sex was only a little less important to him than his music was. Sexuality — *"those glands down there"* — unconsciously permeated everything he did, from his voice to his gestures to his guitar playing. He was serious-minded, even solemn, and yet at the same time, I distinctly sensed that there was an element of madness in his refusal to accept any boundaries whatsoever, sexually or otherwise. He could find erotic possibilities in the least likely situations — the more absurd, the better; the further he could push the envelope, the better he liked it. And all the while he was pushing it, he was laughing...not too loud, but very deeply.

As the tour progressed I was pleasantly surprised to find that Frank was a model roommate. But it made perfect sense. He was a practiced 'road rat'; during the years he'd spent touring he had *To revive the* acquired the hard-won art of graceful, efficient *freshness* living in a vacuum. Well organized and orderly to *of your* *dainty* a fault, he was forever going around picking up *garments* my odds and ends and sorting and arranging them for me. I had never been looked after with such determination, and I found it confusing: On the one hand, I wished he'd ask me first before he took charge of my stuff, but on the other hand, I had to admit I enjoyed the novelty of opening my guitar case and not finding dirty underwear in it. (My slovenly habits must have driven Frank to distraction, but beyond the occasional harrumph, he showed admirable restraint.)

I soon found I had a problem with him making me laugh, although there wasn't much I could do about it. When he wasn't around a group of people, or onstage, he was far from garrulous, but when he did make an observation about something, it was likely to be droll, and all too often his comments had me nearly choking to death, trying not to crack up. One night some no-budget sci-fi opus was showing on the local channel's Red Eye Theater, and Frank sat up in bed improvising cheesy dialogue with the sound off until I finally couldn't stand another second. I begged him to stop, tears rolling down my cheeks.

"Can't take it, huh?" he said, raising a stagily contemptuous eyebrow. But it was too late. I laughed so hard that I literally wound up wetting the sheets. Frank immediately ceased tormenting me and made a wild dash for the other bed, which made me laugh even harder.

Frank's sense of humor extended into areas where others didn't even dare to chuckle: he was the only guy I ever met who could laugh in the throes of the sexual act. Seriously. *"It's all the same muscles relaxing"* (this pronounced with true pseudo-scientific gravity -- *ask Mr. Wizard!*). For him, reproductive organs weren't merely *plumbing*, but *sublime inboard recreational equipment.* "What could you possibly do out there that could be half as entertaining as what we could do in here?" I doubt whether I'll ever be able to wipe from my mind the picture of him standing in shag carpeting up to his knees in some Holiday Inn, not exactly a candidate for the best-dressed list, *right hand from the heart-a*, solemnly reciting the lyrics to an old hokum blues number: "Your balls hang down like a damn bell clapper, your dick stands up like a steeple, your asshole's just like two church doors, and the crabs walk in like people."

Yes -- there was a definite madness in Dr. Zurkon's method, methought.

Even though Frank could be warm and genial in public and considerate and affectionate in private, he made no attempt to dissemble when he was in a bad mood; to him, dishonesty was a far worse sin than possibly offending somebody with a baldly stated or irate comment. The way I figured it, he appeared to be less than genial between a quarter and a third of the time. His emotional barometer would change without warning, and I soon became entirely too familiar with the lowered brows, the sour, confrontational glare, the clipped, sarcastic rejoinders. This state could be brought on by anything — no coffee, not enough sleep, malfunctioning equipment, an interviewer asking the 'wrong' questions — or, seemingly, by nothing at all. It was just his way of handling emotional overload. I rarely felt that Frank's ill humor was directed specifically towards me, but it was still extremely unpleasant. You could feel it building up and hanging in the air like electrostatically charged ozone before a thunderstorm. The minute I saw it coming, I'd get the hell out of the area and watch from a safe distance while some less knowledgeable fool got the downpour; only when I was sure the disturbance had passed did I venture up close again.

I liked him much better when he grinned, slapped his knee in delight at some absurdity, made up ridiculous nicknames for various portions of my anatomy, affectionately twiddled the tip of my nose, suddenly appeared out of nowhere with an unidentified bulbous object in his hand and that look in his eye.

One night, after an especially tiring day, I got back to the motel aching in every muscle. As I stiffly changed out of my clothes, Frank noticed my condition, made me lie down, and proceeded to administer a back rub. Just a few minutes earlier, in the car on the way to the motel, he had been chewing out one of the band members for showing up fifteen minutes late at the sound check that afternoon. Being there while he gave the guy hell had made me extremely uncomfortable; I spent the ride looking studiously out of the window and wishing I'd gone in the other car. Even now, as Frank worked on my back, I was still feeling ill at ease, and he could tell. "You thought I was being an asshole, razzing _____ like that, didn't you?" he asked quietly.

"Sort of," I admitted.

"Well, that's just what you have to do when you're running a band. Next time he would have been half an hour late for the *show*, and then the other guys would've seen him getting away with it and gone, 'Hey, if *he* can be late, *we* can too,' and there you go..."

"Why didn't you just explain that to him quietly, then?"

"I'd already given him a couple of friendly warnings. _____'s not a bad sort of guy, he's just not always that great at paying attention. That's why I had to remind him about it in a way he'd remember. Now roll over..."

"Hmm, I dunno — do I want to be intimate with Mussolini? How do I know I'm not going to be the next one to get it?"

"You're *definitely* going to be the next one to get it. C'mon, roll over."

Frank was an astute psychologist. He understood the personality and peccadilloes of each of the musicians and most of the time he was easily able to motivate them without their being more than dimly aware of it. He knew when to push and when to back off; if I had been in his position, I would have been driven crazy by the swirling cross-currents of band politics, conflicts, neuroses, and high school-level road shenanigans, but Frank had an incredible ability to shrug off the nonsense and effectively deal with what remained. It all fit in with my initial impression when he'd showed me the prospectus for *200 Motels* : he may not have looked the part, but he was a born executive. Although he tried to listen to the band members' complaints and suggestions, he basically didn't give a fig what anybody thought of him, and he never took it personally if a musician decided he hated him and wanted to quit. This, however, was not a regular occurrence; despite the musical discipline he insisted upon, most of his personnel liked and respected him and were willing to give 100 percent, whether or not they alwaysunderstood exactly what they were doing, or why he wanted them to do it.

My troubles with the other band members had commenced almost immediately. The guys, most of them pretty typical rock musicians, were a bunch of pathological socializers, and I wasn't. Worse, my presence as understudy made the dissolute among them, knowing why I was there, regard me with hostility as a prig and a scab. Besides, I was a girl trying to infiltrate their male ranks. Their stage shtick revolved around road humor and groupie jokes — so where did I fit in?

I noticed that the atmosphere of constant partying, both on- and offstage, tended to make Frank more outgoing. He'd hang out with the guys after a show the way somebody else might attend the office cocktail party — although when the action got hot and heavy (as it inevitably did), he rarely took an active role, preferring to leave that to the others. It wasn't that he was beyond arousal — in fact, he walked around in a perpetual state of multi-dimensional sexual awareness that was actually far more dangerous than even the most incorrigible cocksman in the band could conceive of — but he had his own distinct way of viewing things, and in his mind these semi-public orgies were part of his supra-musical megastructure, the 'conceptual continuity' he'd mentioned to me. I think, too, that although he never admitted it, he kept a clear distinction in his mind between himself and his employees. He was their boss and their leader; tactically, there could be no question of him really mingling with them. Abandoning himself to an indiscriminate hot time with a bunch of band members and groupies one night might make it difficult if not impossible for him to maintain his position of control over 'the troops' the next day.

Opportunities for *optional recreational activities* arose constantly in that pre-AIDS epoch, although the typical 'tourist' tended to resemble the young woman in her early 20s, dressed all in rusty black and with raccoon-like black circles painted around each eye, who showed up at a sound check one afternoon and ambushed Frank backstage. "I've been saving *all* my bodily secretions for you for a *month*," she crooned to him.

"That right?" said Frank, giving me a quizzical look over her shoulder. "Is there any particular reason you've singled *me* out for this honor?"

"I just *knew* you'd be able to appreciate them," she gushed. Before she could offer a free sample, Dick Barber was summoned and she was escorted out the fire exit. All that afternoon and evening, Frank kept repeating disgustedly, "She was saving *all* her bodily secretions for me — for a *month*! Oh, *maaaan!...*" He was suddenly no longer Dr. Zurkon, recording psychosexual and anthropological abnormalities for future reference; he was just a *seriously nauseated* guy; a couple of times he actually retched. Frank absolutely despised dirt. He tried to keep his clothes as clean as possible (not always an easy task on the road), and he practically lived in the shower. Even the *concept* of filth (physically, that is) was abhorrent to him. I later heard stories from seemingly reliable sources, alleging that during his early days in the music business, he'd been a veritable Welcome Wagon of venereal afflictions. That was in distinct contradiction to my experience, although, knowing him, anything *could* have been possible.

When less revolting customers showed up and insisted on demonstrating their special talents, he was charming, genial, a bit perverse — he'd invite them up to our room and let them share their abilities freely, if they were so inclined, but afterward he would politely point out that we had to catch a plane at 6:30 the next morning... He was so forthright about these socio-sexual situations that it was hard for me to feel jealous. I found some comfort in the fact that he never dissembled, and that whatever he did, at least he did it in front of me.

Despite his characteristic honesty, he was the victim of a strange little double standard — no matter what *he* did, he tended to exhibit a proprietary attitude toward me, sort of a cross between an overprotective Italian older brother and a jealous boyfriend. He didn't make a show of it, but he was always watching me out of the corner of his eye to make sure I wasn't being too charming to any of the guys in the band. It became readily apparent that the reverse psychology he employed in marketing his persona and music also affected his *personal dynamics*. If I found his attention wandering elsewhere, all I had to do to refocus it was seem to be interested in somebody — anybody — else. Suddenly Frank would materialize out of nowhere, grumbling and glaring and *not going away*. *Whatever was difficult or impossible for him to obtain was precisely what he wanted the most*. I saw this demonstrated very graphically when one of the guys in the band developed a crush on me. He was very sweet, but I only paid attention to him when I needed to get Frank's. Twice was enough. I should have been ashamed.

My performing experience (besides the youth orchestra) up to this point had consisted of private parties, small clubs and coffeehouses, and occasionally somewhat larger venues like the Ascot Raceway in Gardena. Until now, for me an enormous audience had been three or four hundred people.

Thus, when early in the tour I encountered my first *hockey rink* — an outdoor arena with a capacity of about 10,000 — I was instantly seized with an incapacitating terror. As we pulled up near the rear entrance, the huge spotlights were so bright I couldn't tell if there was a full house, but when we were back in the dressing area, the vast, rumbling roar of the crowd made it sound as though even the sky boxes were full.

Frank watched me shaking in my boots, and made a few reassuring comments. Hockey rinks held no fear for him; after all, he'd been touring steadily since 1965. I doubt whether he'd ever felt much stage fright, even at the beginning — the only thing that he disliked about performing (besides malfunctioning equipment or lousy acoustics) was having to sing, and in this group he had plenty of other people to do that for him.

"Hey, you know when they turn the lights up the audience can't even *see* you," he explained. "And with that crappy PA system they can't hear you either. Besides which, most of the members of the audience are probably in an advanced state of *chemical nirvana* anyway. They couldn't care less if you get two notes wrong in that little run there, they're just here to have a good time. What you got to be nervous about?" I looked at the reflection in the fingerprint-smudged mirror in front of us, there in that makeshift dressing room that reeked of second-hand beer and sour, athletic sweat. I saw myself, white as a sheet, desperately clutching the red SG, and beside me Frank, cool and collected with his black Les Paul, a fresh cigarette stuck in the pegboard. The opening band had finished its set, and out in the bleachers the crowd was clapping, stamping, whistling, and shouting for *us*. I could feel the concrete floor vibrating with their enthusiasm.

"Come on," said Frank. "Let's go *entertain* them."

There was a concrete tunnel linking the dressing area to the stage. Frank went first, with his characteristic purposeful stride; I was behind him, and the rest of the band followed us. As we approached the end of the tunnel the crowd noise became deafening. A short flight of steps led up to the stage. Walking to the front of the stage, the plywood creaked under my boots; my knees were shaking, and my mouth was so dry I couldn't have spit to save my life. From the rigging overhead, the spots threw huge hot sheets of daylight right down into our faces, making it impossible to see out into the crowd. I felt like I was climbing up to the gallows — how could Frank be so nonchalant? There he was, stealing a puff of his cigarette, adjusting the tuner on his B string, trying the harmonic, clearing his throat -- all the while looking as cozy as if he were in his own living room. *"Hello, boys 'n' girls,"* he greeted the crowd, which responded with a cheer that felt like a 9.6 earthquake. "Could you please turn up the monitor?" he asked the sound reinforcement guys at the mixing board.

When he counted off the first song, my fingers refused to move. I got them around the guitar neck finally, and began to play, although my shaking hand was applying an inadvertent tremelo. The song progressed, and slowly I began to feel a dull amazement: why, I was still alive, and even more amazing, I actually remembered my parts.

By the end of the number I was almost enjoying myself. After the first show I'd begun to understand the intense decibel level a rock band generated, and I'd quickly picked up some ear plugs, but this wasn't the same as playing in an auditorium. In fact, performing for 10,000 people in a hockey rink was practically an anonymous act — Frank was right; they couldn't really see you or hear you. Nor could you see or hear anything yourself. It was like being blind and deaf, with an audience that was also blind and deaf. The relentless pounding of the bass and drums was all that came through, and I felt *that* in my gut, rather than hearing it through my ears. It was quite strange to realize that when I played a lead, I was the only person in the whole arena who knew whether it was any good or not. Even Frank couldn't hear clearly enough to tell if I were playing Hindemith or "Louie Louie". Hey, this was fun. No wonder rock 'n' roll musicians swaggered and strutted around on stage — most of them were getting away with *murder* up there.

Frank looked out for me in a lot of little ways. There was a quaint, charming quality in the way he fussed over details for my benefit — although I never would have dared to tell him I thought it was quaint and charming. He knew that I had a tendency to lose guitar picks, and he always kept a bunch of them handy for me, pulling them out of his guitar case with an exaggerated flourish, a shake of the head, and an affectionate "Oh man are you ever *hopeless*." He observed that I was often too distracted to remember to eat, and cheeseburgers (no mayo, ketchup, or mustard, onions only) would magically appear at my elbow.

One night I ripped my best shirt half an hour before we had to leave for the show. I began melodramatically howling that now I would have to go onstage naked (actually I could have borrowed one of Frank's numerous T-shirts — I'd been doing that a lot because I hadn't brought nearly enough changes of clothes). Frank came over, frowned in his mock-paternal way, and examined the damage. "Gimme that," he ordered, and crossing over to his suitcase he pulled out a tiny sewing kit, sat down on the edge of the bed, and squinting under the bedside lamp, proceeded to stitch away on my injured garment, looking like a mutant version of some old Sicilian immigrant tailor. He handed back my shirt a few minutes later with a smug little gesture. I looked for the torn spot, but in vain. The stitches were so small and neat that the repair was practically invisible; his sewing was more skillfully executed than most women's. I don't know why this surprised me, but it did. (*Real men don't sew...?*) Later he explained that he'd learned to sew as a kid when he'd built his own puppet theater and made elaborate costumes for all the characters. He was still putting on puppet shows, only now, like the Puppetmaster in *Petrouchka*, he was using live marionettes, and sometimes *we* also needed our stage clothes sewed.

For *This* I Learned to Play Stravinsky??!

He was acutely sensitive toward me without being dramatic about it. When he could see that the relentless pace of constant travel on too little sleep, or the steady barrage of sensations, was about to make me blow a fuse, he would put his arm around me and hold me close to him, not belaboring me with further talk or stimulation, his reassurance eloquent in its calm silence. Finally he'd ask simply, "You OK now?" I usually was. Once, when I was feeling miserably homesick and low-spirited, he cut short a phone interview so he could take me out for lunch. This was entirely out of character for him; he was somewhat agoraphobic, and he tried to avoid social situations whenever he could because he loathed the inane chitchat that inevitably accompanied things like eating in restaurants. That particular afternoon, though, he was affectionate, funny in his inimitable way, and altogether comforting. When we got back to our room, he hung out the DO NOT DISTURB sign, and by showtime that night, the whole concept of homesickness had completely ceased to be relevant.

I definitely needed reassuring sometimes. Frank's nature was to blow things up, blast them wide open; and he understood that I, in my closed-off state, was attracted to him because I somehow realized that. But as strange as it may seem, he also had a pronounced sense of responsibility, and I think he felt uneasy at the intensity of my reactions, knowing he'd stirred them up. He knew he shouldn't be playing with that sort of dynamite, however thrilling the explosion was. I had a feeling, too, that he was afraid the situation would force a reaction from him — one that he was entirely unprepared to confront, much less control.

Sex he could handle, because it was exciting and interesting; love, on the other hand, was a different matter. From things he said, or almost said, I gathered that his first marriage and a couple of his other relationships had ended badly because the women in question hadn't understood his need for freedom. Frank could be loyal, but he wasn't cut out for monogamy; it went too much against his essentially polymorphous nature, and besides, it sounded too much like that *other* word, 'monotony.' In another way, the conventional notion of romance probably seemed absurd and contemptible to him because of its one-dimensionality. Poor Frank. I could never have said it to his face, but he was actually a romantic, if you blast open the standard definition of romanticism and take another look at it as *an unrealistically expansive view of human relationships.* Nobody could live up to that sort of expectation — not even Frank himself.

For him, *love* was a transitive verb, not some flowery adjec-

47

tive. *Lust* was a concept he understood perfectly; its adjunct was *improvisation,* and the desired result was *adventure,* or at least diversion. And yet he was far more giving than selfish. Being instinctively attentive to detail, he generally succeeded admirably in defining the precise point of pleasurability and would then proceed to attack it with a frankly degenerate gusto.

He was such a realist — or a cynic — that he couldn't really comprehend the fact that I appreciated him simply for himself — not because he was a *Guitar Hero,* a *Ticket Out of Oblivion,* or a *Sort of a Father Figure.* Actually, it hadn't taken me long to recognize that although we were of different gender and from different eras and family backgrounds, Frank and I had something profound and not a little ironic in common. We were both eccentrics; for some reason we had wound up being different than everybody else, but our thought patterns and reactions were very similar. Of course most serious Mothers fans were weirdos to a greater or lesser extent, but the more familiar I became with Frank's music, the more I began to understand why it spoke so eloquently to me: It mirrored my own emotions and perceptions on a deep, unconscious level. The only other composer whose music felt that emotionally familiar to me was Erik Satie — another iconoclast and joker who was always conscious of his outsider status.

When I played the music, I had the feeling of being 'plugged into' something I didn't understand, a level of simultaneous reality Frank hadn't invented himself but had somehow tapped into. I had sensed this amorphous but pervasive atmosphere when I'd first met him, and when later he told me that, like me, he had read his share of books on Zen, it made a lot of sense. Frank seemed to understand the concept of Zen well enough: it was a state you simply lived in — or didn't. Because we were both together so much, I moved more into that state as the tour went on.

Early in the tour I began to have 'coincidental' experiences with Frank that bordered on being eerie. At one of the shows where I didn't perform, he introduced the world premiere of a new song and explained to the audience that it was extremely difficult to execute. I was standing behind the amps, watching, and I grinned to myself and said under my breath, "Which is no doubt why you're not going to play on it." At that moment, Frank announced, "Which is why I'm not going to play on it."

Another time we were trading guitar solos over a vamp in A. I took my allotted solo space, then Frank took his. At the end of his solo we vamped for eight bars, then all of a sudden, without any warning, we both launched into an identical eight-bar phrase together, in perfect rhythm! It sounded as tight as if we'd rehearsed it. We exchanged a bemused glance across the stage, and Frank frowned a little, like I'd tried to put something over on him. Afterward I asked him if he'd ever played that lick before, thinking maybe I'd heard him toss it off once and had then 'forgotten' it, but he claimed he hadn't — in fact, he said, it had been rhythmically and harmonically alien to his style, and he'd felt almost peculiar when he played it. I could almost hear the theme from "The Twilight Zone". We experienced a number of these 'coincidences' during the time we knew each other.

As little as I actually performed with him, I learned more about guitar playing from Frank in that period than I probably would have learned from 20 years with any other guitarist: his understanding of *when* to play *what* was absolute. He wasn't some athletic guitar god like

Jimmy Page or Eric Clapton; in fact, he always looked a little klutzy onstage, one shoulder higher than the other from the weight of his Les Paul or Strat, the eternal burning cigarette stuck under the strings on the pegboard — and so, when he fired off an intricate lead in Hungarian

49

minor (neatly swiped from the first movement of Bartok's Third Piano Concerto), ornamented with a wreath of perfectly executed hair's-breadth spacings (17 against 13, borrowed from Stravinsky and probably never repaid), it always seemed like a lucky accident. How could this guy, who generally looked like he was *truly hurting* for a square meal and a good night's sleep, come blasting out with something so concise, so humorous, so downright unthinkable? "Do it again, Frank!" I'd yell — and he'd give me a look over his shoulder, wonderfully arrogant, like a little wink: "Of *course* we'll play *Petrouchka* ..." And then he'd fling out another solo for nothing — ten, or a thousand, times better than the first one.

Although it sounded like it was a product of the 'psychedelic' era, Frank's style of guitar playing actually went back much farther than that; it was a strange but effective amalgamation of a blues skeleton fleshed out with harmonies and rhythms from 20th-century orchestral music. No matter how complex his playing was rhythmically and harmonically, in some sense Frank never strayed far from his bluesy roots. When after the tour I got around to hearing some very early, pre-Mothers of Invention tapes of Frank playing in a straightforward blues style, my impression was that the his 1962 guitar persona could have stepped right onstage with the 1971 version, and wouldn't have really sounded any different. As far back as 1962, all the things I associated with the Zappa style — the rhythmic emphasis, his tendency to finger more notes than he picked, the modal quality of his playing, and above all the essential honesty of his playing — were all there. His guitar style was fully formed by the time he was in his early 20s; the only thing that changed over the years was the price of his toys — the instruments themselves and the amplifier and effects technology. He used to amaze impressionable listeners by playing the main themes to *Petrouchka* and *The Rite of Spring*, first individually and then together, in the form of a canon, but what the audience didn't realize was that he'd been doing that musical stunt for years — on one of those early tapes, in fact, was a recording of a blues jam in which he'd shoehorned in the Stravinsky guitar trick after an endless harmonica solo. It didn't really work in that context, but I don't think it was supposed to.

You could always tell when he'd memorized a part and was playing it by rote — he played it precisely, but a little painfully, as though it were an exercise. For instance, he had arranged the first few bars of the trumpet fanfare from Stravinsky's *Agon* and inserted it into his song "Status Back Baby". He had more trouble fingering that obstinate little tidbit than he wanted to admit. One night back at the motel I did something that only a callous 17-year-old would have thought was humorous: we were running through some material, and he took a break to go to the bathroom, leaving the door open. Meanwhile, I cheerfully tossed off the break from *Agon* three or four times as if it were the merest trifle, messing with the rhythm and generally showing off. When Frank came back, he gave me such a sour, cranky look that I cracked up.

He didn't say anything, but the next time the song came up at a show, he made a big deal out of stopping right at that point, then grandiosely announced to the audience that I was going to perform the trumpet fanfare from *Agon* on the guitar *unaccompanied* and *totally amaze them.* I was thrown into total confusion; I'd never thought I'd be doing it *in public* . Naturally, I fucked it up. Frank thought it was so hilarious he stood there and made me play it *again.* The second time was even worse than the first. After that I evinced a little more *respect* for his limitations.

Frank had developed a beautiful and highly unusual harmonic sense, both chordally and in the melodic patterns he soloed on, but the most important element in his playing was always rhythm. When he soloed, his rhythms tended to fall into odd patterns — 3s, 5s, 7s, 9s — over the basic 4/4 rock pulse. It reminded me of Indian music, with the lengthy, irregular solo line rolling out over and often against several cycles of structured rhythm. After hearing him, I had trouble listening to other guitarists; most of them tended to sound dull and predictable by comparison, and their rhythmic sense seemed so rudimentary. But it was something else, some elusive quality, that set Frank apart from the ranks of rock guitar abusers. There were other guitarists who could play faster, cleaner, more glibly than Frank, but none of them came close to his 'attitude' — that steamy, palpable sense of immediacy. His guitar playing had both intellectual and visceral qualities, although he probably didn't separate one from the other, any more than he differentiated between Edgard Varèse and Guitar Slim. It was all just part of his composition. For Frank, playing the guitar was never a job, a cut-and-dried activity; it was an adventure and a release, like sex but much better, a brief span of time when he could close his eyes, figuratively speaking, and jump off into the void. He had the power to draw the listener into his musical world and hold them there, expanding and ultimately suspending all sense of time.

When it came to his music, he knew exactly what he wanted, and he wouldn't accept anything less. He assumed the musicians he hired were going to work as hard as he did, and if somebody couldn't or wouldn't deliver, they were excused without further dithering. He didn't have that trouble with me; but (beyond the confusing aspects of our mutating relationship) there were definite areas where our musical philosophies crashed head-on.

Frank had done too much hard time in bars and lounges in industrial suburbs, playing watered-down versions of Tin Pan Alley banalities with hopeless rhythm sections for the delectation of sodden oafs; so when I'd throw in a flat-five substitution, he'd wince and proceed to fulminate on the banality of musical evil, deriding the sterility of *white people's music* . In the Antelope Valley in the '50s he had been jailed the night before a dance because he had led a racially mixed R&B band; the local Okies thought all niggers were dope fiends and gangsters. Italians were considered pretty alien by the hayseeds in Lancaster, and Frank had suffered miserably in high school at the hands of the second-generation Okie and Arkie students. There was no point in my trying to explain to him that there were plenty of outcasts in places like Texas and Oklahoma, and as much innovation in Spade Cooley as there was in Anton Webern. Frank didn't have many deep prejudices, but the ones he had seemed to have been burned into his soul with an excoriating lash.

Gender may have been one of his unconscious prejudices, though he didn't seem overtly sexist. Even so, his misplaced sense of propriety may have been *one* of the reasons why our collaboration was so brief. There *weren't* many women guitarists in the early '70s, at least not blatant lead players. Frank had worked with a guitarist named Alice Stuart back in the beginning, but he told me she had been a folky, fingerstyle player; he said he'd fired her because she couldn't play "Louie Louie". My basic impulses came from years of listening to damn-the-torpedoes Western swing and hot jazz records, which gave my playing a raw, aggressive, unpredictable edge. Frank was intrigued by it, but he was also a bit put off; he was always trying to get me to play even 'uglier', in a distorted-signal, screeching-feedback sense, but when I did, he couldn't quite handle it — maybe the picture of a *young lady beating the shit out of an electric guitar* wasn't really something he wanted to see. Once he asked, "Doesn't having that thing [i.e., the guitar] strapped on to you hurt your tits?" He was being facetious, in his inimitable way, but I sensed that what he was really saying was, *What's a nice girl like you doing with a **thing** like that?* Hopefully not upstaging *him*.

Sometimes he'd just talk about music. He lived and breathed it, and a casual question from me was likely to elicit a flood of stories and free association. I wish I'd made tapes of some of those discussions, like the one where he described how during the 1930s Edgard Varèse had quit composing for almost 25 years, partly because at that point musical technology hadn't caught up to him yet, but also because he was depressed and discouraged at the way his music was being received. From there the conversation somehow drifted to the subject of underdogs. When he'd spent a brief period in jail in San Bernardino, Frank told me, he had sat there, powerless to do anything but fume over the injustices of the legal system and think about playing the guitar. He said he'd fantasized about playing guitar chords so loud and ugly that they'd tear the rebar right out of the cement-block walls and blast him to freedom. No wonder he'd always been so fond of Johnny "Guitar" Watson's early record "Three Hours Past Midnight" — the one where the guitar solos resembled a barrage of machine-gun fire. In Frank's lengthy opus "Joe's Garage," recorded in the late '70s, Joe, the guitar-playing protagonist, is jailed because musicians are perceived as a threat to society. There, stuck in his cell, he dreams of playing monstrous lines on the guitar as a form of revenge against his captors. They can't control his thoughts, and they especially can't do anything about his imaginary guitar playing.

Any idiot could see that Frank fought against restraints of any kind with every ounce of his will. Just a hint that someone or something was about to confine or limit him was enough to make him start imploding with outrage. On one level, he rejected boundaries: musical, sexual, or political; more prosaically, he refused to wear a watch, saying, with strange symbolism, that it hampered his guitar playing. He always slept naked, and when he wasn't going out of the motel room he generally had his shirt off; if it was warm enough, he shucked his pants as well.

I couldn't own him, but since I was borrowing him so often, the distinction was pretty well lost on me.

Situations arose regularly which put me in an awkward position. One afternoon during a lengthy sound check, Frank was making the band go over and over one eight-bar section of a song; the rhythm section was being especially obtuse. I was sitting in a folding chair on one side of the stage when one of the musicians' girlfriends came up to me and said artlessly, "You know, Nigey, Frank's guitar is so loud it's drowning out everybody else. He'll listen to *you* — why don't you go over there and tell him to turn down a little?" I guess they wanted to set me and Frank against each other, hoping to get me kicked off the tour. I didn't give them the satisfaction. Had I not been involved with Frank, I would probably have been trying to organize the musicians, anarcho-syndicalist that I am, but given the potential for conflict of interest, I tried to stay out of politics.

On another occasion, there was a party going on in our room after a show. Leaving the revelers to revel, I slipped into the shower. When I got out, I decided I needed a Coke from the hall machine, which was located not more than 20 feet away from the door of the room. It was pretty late, and since I was warm and steamy from the shower, I decided to run out and grab the Coke clad only in a minuscule bath towel, figuring I'd run back into the bathroom and get dressed afterwards, before anybody had a chance to even notice. They were all fairly well preoccupied, it seemed to me.

I dashed out into the hall and obtained the beverage (the machine was out of everything but ginger ale, but that was OK: for some reason Frank often had a pagan craving for warm, flat Schweppes — *"the universal solvent"*) , and then I raced back to the door and turned the knob. I'd left it unlocked, but suddenly I heard the deadbolt shoot closed inside. And there I was, locked out, my undignified posterior playing peek-a-boo from under that green logo, in the hallway of a godforsaken Holiday Inn in the wee small hours of oblivion — some pre-anthropoid road rat's idea of a joke. Of course it had never occurred to me to take the key with me. *Har, har, har.* I stood there pounding on the door and muttering, incoherent with rage. Anyone who had seen me at that moment would have taken me for a madwoman, with my long dripping hair, extremely casual garb, and demented expression. But at least nobody *would* see me — all the world was safe in bed at that hour.

As fate would have it, just then I heard footsteps coming toward me down the hall. I pressed myself flat against the door, wishing I were the Incredible Shrinking Woman, or that I could be instantly turned into a pumpkin. No dice. Here were the young, painfully straight-looking couple from the room next door, trying valiantly not to stare at me in all my glory while thinking, no doubt, that the lurid tales they'd half-heard about traveling rock 'n' roll bands were vastly understated. A wild non sequitur raced through my mind: *For this I learned to play Stravinsky??!*

At the same instant, the door to the room burst open without warning, and I came close to breaking my neck as I fell inside. Inside, everybody was rolling around on the floor, braying like jackasses. Frank,

assuming his role of disciplinarian, feebly attempted to issue a stern rejoinder to the culprits, but even he broke down in the middle and was unable to continue.

As my understanding of him developed, I began to realize that in a surprising number of ways, Frank Zappa was all about the 19th century, not, as nearly anyone would have thought, the mid-20th-century. (When I was able to take a look around *Chez* Zappa, I wasn't at all surprised to find that it had a formal parlor with a bunch of knickknacks on the mantel, Tiffany lamps, quaint chairs, ugly upholstery, and a strong feeling of stuffy propriety despite its psychedelic purple walls.) The battles, sexual and musical, Frank was fighting were Victorian: his musical heroes Stravinsky, Webern, and Varèse had all been born in the 19th century and had struggled to throw off the shackles of 19th-century musical convention, albeit each in a different way. Even Frank's obsession with technology was Victorian, as was his droll, largely verbal sense of humor. He claimed not to be much of a reader, but his vocabulary was so flexible and precise, not to mention picturesque, that it gave him away as an audodidact, whether he liked it or not. I imagine that, growing up as the first-generation child of immigrant parents, he had absorbed their 19th-century European attitudes. In fact, he was scornful of everything

American — beer, sports, Manifest Destiny, you name it.

When I heard about his first visit to Europe on tour with the band a few years earlier, I gathered it had been something of an epiphany for him to walk through the streets of Vienna and see Webern's musical scores in shop windows, or to stop by a cafe where people sat around all day doing nothing but reading newspapers and talking politics. As an instinctive intellectual mired in a crass commercial culture, he was struggling like *The Fly* — "Help me! Help me!" He had been condemned, whether he really knew it or not, to *Life in the Wrong Era* — he belonged in *belle époque* Paris, or Berlin in the '20s, not "I Like Ike" America. I'd survived high school by immersing myself in the proto-Dadaist writings of French madman Alfred Jarry, and had daydreamed about being the star of literary and musical orgies in *fin-du-siécle* Paris; while as a 15-year-old exile in the Great American Desert, Frank had similarly fantasized about what it would have been like to pal around with Varèse in Greenwich Village around the time of the Armory Show.

Although I shared with Frank the eccentricity of being brought up at least nominally in the vicinity of Victorian values, unlike him I didn't feel smothered by them. What had attracted me to him was the dimly perceived sense that we had those values in common; when it came to our reactions to them, however, we were bound to clash.

In true Victorian fashion, Frank kept his emotions under tight control, at least most of the time. He seemed to be a private person who had been forced to adapt to life in the limelight by circumstance; as a rugged individual in a conformist world, he had reached the conclusion that his survival hinged on selling the public on his peculiar art by using reverse psychology, exaggerating his 'unsavory' qualities. It worked, but it took its toll on him. He would have preferred to stay home and work on his music, but instead here he was on the road, with brain damaged college kids asking him if he'd ever eaten shit on stage and concert promoters coming up with science fiction figures when they 'counted the house'. He hated interviews and small talk, but on tour his day was made up of almost nothing but both. He was fond of me, I could tell — maybe even more than that — and yet when I looked at the chain of events that led up to my being here with him at this point in time, I had to admit that I was really only a member of that same old public — I just happened to be able to play the guitar. When I thought what it would have been like to have his undivided attention, I began fervently wishing that I was ten years older and that I'd met him in another universe entirely — someplace like the produce section of the Thriftimart in Cucamonga

in 1962, when he was still just the village outcast, not yet a highly tout-
ed *MENACE TO AMERICAN YOUTH.* Of course no one *person* ever
received Frank's undivided attention. That was reserved solely for his work.
It didn't seem to bother him that on the road, sex became an activity
squeezed into the 'window' between the sound check and the gig, or before
the ride to the airport at 5:30 a.m. I tried not to think about how much
he could have delivered if just once he turned his whole mind to it --
but that was dangerous ground, and I knew it. I was beginning to understand that I couldn't surmount the obstacles of a relationship with Frank
Zappa, as much as I wished the truth were otherwise.

    Throughout the whole experience I found myself wondering, log-
ically enough, where exactly the boundaries were in our relationship. I'd
never suspected (*"Who could imagine?"*...) that this off-the-wall tour situation would wind up throwing me and Frank together, with the consequences to both of us; although it's hard to believe Frank hadn't fore-
seen what was likely to happen. Initially I had wanted simply — out of
morbid, embarrassed adolescent curiosity — to find out what kind of a
lover my musical hero was. Now, weeks later, I wasn't much closer to
knowing the answer, but things had gone so far beyond that point that
I didn't care anymore. I just wanted to keep experiencing Frank's universe. There wasn't any way to describe the way I felt about him; our relationship was intense, volatile, stimulating, contradictory, and exhilarating
by turns.

    Since I couldn't begin to understand my feelings toward him, I
was at a loss as to how to behave, so, in typical adolescent fashion, I
largely retreated behind a wisecracking, sarcastic facade. Ironically, Frank,
although he had no use for hearts 'n' flowers niceties, sought emotional
honesty in his relationships, or thought he did, and he was bothered
because he suspected I was holding out on him. I couldn't bring myself
to treat him like a human being. I knew this, but something was holding
me back from trusting him. It was partly because he had been my musical idol long before I'd met him, and partly bound up with my fierce desire
to maintain my dignity as a musician; above all else I craved Frank's
respect. Somehow I was afraid to come right out and admit to him what
he undoubtedly already knew -- that I was horribly in love with him, as
only a 17-year-old can be. The situation would have been difficult enough
even if I'd been older and wiser; and for all my strong will and creative
precocity, I was a pretty emotionally undeveloped 17-year-old.

    For his own part Frank, who was so accustomed to maintaining
control over the situation around him, couldn't decide what he should

do with me: educate me or debauch me. What a choice — frustration or incest. For the time being, the latter won out, but Frank had other concerns. After all, he had a wife and kids to go home to; it wasn't as if I was going to be moving in with him at the end of the tour. Then there was the pesky point of my being underage. Frank had done his jail time in San Bernardino in 1963 on a set-up morals charge — "conspiracy to commit pornography" was the verdict; as the proprietor of a little recording studio in Cucamonga, he'd made the mistake of producing an X-rated "party tape" for a guy who turned out to be an undercover vice cop. One of the conditions of his parole had been that he couldn't fraternize with an underage female unless a "responsible adult" was present. I would have died rather than admit that I was still a minor, but I'm sure that fact was never far from his mind.

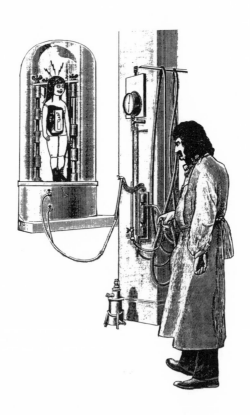

CHAPTER 6

Positively 57th Street

A s Frank had mentioned before I joined the tour, the band had been on the road for the best part of six months by the time I came on board. It didn't take me long to understand what he meant by "battle fatigue." For a week or two, it may seem like an adventure to go from city to city playing a concert every night, but after a month every place starts looking the same, and after two months utter psychosis sets in.

Frank was far from robust physically, and endless touring was probably the worst punishment he could have inflicted on himself. He may have expressed an aversion to drugs, but that didn't stop him from chain smoking three or four packs a day, guzzling gallons of coffee, and adopting a devil-may-care approach to diet. One of the guys in the band was on a macrobiotic kick, and he carried a rice cooker with him so he could always have brown rice and tamari. Frank thought this was very quaint, almost religious. His own culinary theology revolved around the mantra: "Whatever it is, *fry it first and ask questions later.*" He constantly suffered with stomach troubles and bouts of diarrhea, and was forced to consume gallons of Kaopectate and Maalox.

I'd always thought I was quirkier about food than most people — until I had to turn the trophy over to Frank. One day at the airport, with our flight due to leave in fifteen minutes, I left him watching the luggage and ran to grab a couple of sandwiches from the fast-food counter. Up until now I'd never had to actually order anything for him, and I decided to play it safe and stick to turkey and lettuce on rye. When I got back to the waiting area and handed him his sandwich, he opened its sheet of wax paper, took apart the two pieces of bread, and proceeded to poke around minutely in the filling before committing himself to a bite. Suddenly his probing finger encountered a few little slivers of chopped onion, and before my incredulous eyes he was instantly transformed into Superman in a petulant frenzy: what was I trying to do, *stuff him with Kryptonite when he wasn't looking??!* I sat there in disbelief, trying not to laugh, as he chucked the sandwich, wrapper and all, into the nearest garbage can, all the while keeping up a scathing commentary on the villainies of (allegedly) edible bulbs. Frank also actively disproved my long-held theory that people of Mediterranean ancestry had evolved a garlic gene. He had about as much fondness for garlic as he had for onions. In fact, when it came to any sort of Italian-type food (with the lone exception of pizza), he exhibited a pronounced *attitude*. I once offered him a bite of lasagna in a coffee shop. He looked queasily at the ricotta and sauce dribbling off my fork and said weakly, "Looks authentic." Now if I'd spiced it with tobacco and coffee grounds first, I could probably have induced him to eat the whole thing. What he *really* lusted after was peanut butter, with or without anchovies.

The worst thing about touring was the *Day of the Living Dead Syndrome*. I had never been a heavy sleeper, but five or six hours a night was my bare minimum. Frank needed closer to ten. We were lucky to average three. After a month or so, I decided that the standard media picture of him as a scowling misanthrope had been shot at 6 a.m. in an airport waiting area when the Kaopectate had run out. I felt sorry for him, but I couldn't really understand why he spent such a disproportionate chunk of his life suffering like that, especially since there was minimal profit in touring; the only reason he was out there playing hockey rinks in Peoria was because he had to promote his latest album, and now his new movie. It was only much later that I realized why he did it. He sold more records if he kept his profile up, but touring fulfilled another function for him too: it was both a great source of material and it provided a strong contrast to his life at home, which tended to be comfortable but insular — the kiss of death for such a topical composer as Frank was. At home, he virtually never went out, preferring to sequester himself in his own reality, staying up all night working and sleeping during the day. He needed stimulation and inspiration, and touring was the only way for him to meet people and get a feeling for what was going on in the world. (Later in his life, when he no longer had the financial compulsion to tour, and middle age had rendered him physically and emotionally less capable of the exertion, he became addicted to C-SPAN and Cable News Network, but for much the same reason.)

He had devised ways of making use of the inevitable stretches of dead time. While sitting around a motel room or waiting for a flight at the airport, he'd haul out his orchestra pad and start composing on the spot, staring into space and tapping his foot to private rhythms, his left hand in sync on his knee. I wondered what he could actually *hear* when he did it, but he had written a fair amount of music that way, including the entire score to *200 Motels* (hence the title). As he jerked the pen along the staff, drawing clusters of precisely spaced little dots and linking them with crossbars and 'tuplet ligatures, he was as happy as I ever saw him — in public, anyway. He had been a commercial artist for awhile, before music had sunk its permanent hooks into him. I wasn't sure he recognized any boundaries between graphics and music, any more than he made value judgments about Varèse or Stravinsky being "better" than the Penguins or Guitar Slim. It was all part of the ongoing process of his work — his "composition", as he called it.

Frank wasn't exactly clumsy, but he tended to be the catalyst for improbable accidents. One bleary morning when we were driving to the airport, guzzling dubious Holiday Inn coffee in a futile attempt to stay awake, the lid popped off Frank's styrofoam cup and I was baptized in 12 ounces of scalding tan water. That certainly woke me up. In agony I lurched and writhed across the back seat of the station wagon, howling at the top of my lungs as the hot fluid penetrated my T-shirt. As I writhed, I inadvertently kicked the hell out of Frank's shin with the toe of one of my cowboy boots.

He had been solicitously trying to conduct mop-up operations on my torso, but when I booted him he doubled over in pain, jabbing his elbow into my ribs and upsetting *my* cup of coffee, the contents of which came rushing out to join the first cup — on my already soaked shirt. I wound up with some awfully nice blisters, and Frank went scowling around with a noticeable limp. (I don't know what the other band members thought we'd been up to, but their theories about us were always pretty colorful.) Meanwhile, Frank and I conversed in irate grunts during the remainder of the day; each of us was convinced that the whole mishap was solely the fault of the other. Frank grumbled that if I'd been wearing decent, civilized shoes instead of those *barbaric poot-stompers*, he wouldn't have been so badly crippled, while I nattered back that only a *caffeine junkie with a terminal jones* would have been trying to get a fix in a moving car at six in the fucking *morning*.

The tour ground on, ebbing and flowing like a perverse river. At that point, in the early '70s, Frank Zappa occupied a position in the high-middle level of touring rock acts; his arrival in town elicited some fanfare, but the truth (some would say farce) nevertheless remained that bands like Three Dog Night or Ten Years After could far outstrip him in ticket revenues. In several cases, the bands that opened for Frank were better known locally than the Mothers were; after these local fave raves finished their sets, a lot of audience members would listen to the Mothers for a few minutes, decide they didn't like them, and split, leaving Frank and company staring out at a vast landscape of vacant seats while performing.

The venues tended to be War Memorial Halls, college auditoriums, municipal theaters, and, of course, hockey rinks. I hadn't brought along very much of a wardrobe; luckily for me, Frank seemed to have packed every piece of clothing he owned, and so, although I had to roll up the legs of his jeans, I never wanted for raiment. (When during the writing of this book I was looking through old photos of him, I found one in which he was wearing the particular pair of tie-dyed Levi's I had borrowed the most often. My first thought was, *"How the hell could I have ever squeezed into those damn things?"*) On some especially cold nights we bickered over which of us got to wear *The Ugliest Overcoat in the Universe*, a wonderfully stodgy Donegal tweed monstrosity (women's size 18, according to the faded tag inside) to the gig. Being both more cold-blooded and more dogged than I, he usual-

ly won, but then he'd take pity on me, ransack his luggage for a couple of his warmest sweaters, and insist that I put them on. It became quite a joke between us, although it didn't stay private: After the band members had seen me shuffling around in Frank's clothes for a few weeks, a couple of them began to make wisecracks, kidding on the square: "Hi, Frank — oh, sorry, Nigey, I didn't know it was you for a second there." Frank, ever the old pragmatist, advised me not to pay any attention. "Sticks and stones...just be glad they're not pouring lukewarm beer over your head."

Post-show optional recreation tended to be scanty in the hinterlands, but Frank didn't seem to mind, because a relatively early evening meant he could catch up on his sleep. Sometimes, victimized by caffeine, he'd read for awhile, lying there with his arm around me and his book propped up on his chest. (Out of a strange reluctance to appear intellectual, he pretended that he never read anything he didn't absolutely have to read, but one of the first long conversations we had on the tour was about Franz Kafka; Frank seemed to be thoroughly familiar with everything Kafka had ever written, even obscure things like "A Country Doctor".) If I happened to be restless, he'd ignore my flailing about as long as he could and then finally look at me sideways and inquire, "Are you in torment? Well, we certainly can't have that, now can we?" It was a running gag — him always making it seem like it was *my* idea.

One night neither of us could sleep. Nothing helped, not even the old reliable. After thrashing around for awhile we finally gave up and lay there in the dark. Gradually a conversation of sorts evolved, ramblingly and desultorily, lit by the tip of his burning cigarette. I had always wanted to know what his high school days had really been like, and he replied unhesitatingly that adolescence had been the most miserable period of his life. He admitted that when he was 14 or 15 he would have given anything for someone to come along, male or female, who really understood him. "Of course that would have been impossible — I didn't even understand myself," he said with a self-deprecating laugh.

Since he seemed to be in an uncharacteristically self-revelatory mood, and since I'd always been curious, I asked him about the circumstances surrounding his loss of virginity. A tone came into his voice that I had never heard before; even though he was talking in his usual precise, slightly derisive manner of speech, all of a sudden it was like listening to a muted cello playing in a minor key. He had been in high school in Lancaster in the Mojave Desert, a gangly kid with a scraggly mustache, the school outcast. His only friend then was Don Van Vliet (later known as Captain Beefheart), even more of an outcast and weirdo than Frank was. The two of them would listen to blues records all night, and when they got really bored, they'd cruise around Lancaster in Van Vliet's Oldsmobile, looking for girls (this said with a contemptuous little snort, as if it was a deranged notion to think two rejects like *them* would ever find female companionship by cruising the streets of Lancaster in the 1950s). Still, evidently, Frank finally had some luck. "It was at her house when her parents weren't home; at my house either my mother or my brothers and my sister were always around. It was really putrid — neither of us had the vaguest notion what

63

to do, of course. I never saw her afterward — for some reason she never wanted to talk to me again." The outflow of clipped speech stopped suddenly as he laughed, with intense bitterness. I was surprised at the self-hatred that laugh revealed. I began to comprehend why he'd been able to understand me so quickly at our first meeting.

He quickly started asking me questions, turning the tables and trying to regain control. In my high school days, had I ever had sex with a bunch of guys at the same time? How about in public? Had I ever had any mutant lusts — attractions for, say, animals, vegetables, or household appliances? I couldn't bring myself to admit that I'd practically been a virgin until recently. Besides, nothing I could say was as revelatory as what he'd just confessed to me.

I sensed that his childhood and adolescence had been pinched and dreary. He had spent his early childhood in government housing in Maryland; his father was, among other things, a weapons tester for the government arsenal in Edgewood, and had often brought home noxious substances for human testing on his family because the tests meant extra pay, a sorely needed commodity with all those kids to feed. For a long time, said Frank, there had actually been *a big bag of DDT stashed in the hall closet.* "They said you could *eat it* if you wanted to — it was only supposed to kill bugs, and, ostensibly, alien armies."

The next day Frank wouldn't look me in the eye, and when he spoke to me at all, it was in icy monosyllables. I don't think he was ever free of self-consciousness, and by letting his guard down and allowing me a glimpse, however fleeting, of his life in the period when he'd been at the mercy of other people's perceptions of him, he evidently felt he'd lost control — something that was unthinkable to him, because he equated control with freedom. But I suspect he'd been just plain embarrassed, too, and that embarrassed him even more, hence his savagery toward himself for coming out and admitting that shit in the first place. Although he had a great deal of self-respect, there was some part of himself that he hated. He was, hands down, harder on himself than anyone I've ever met.

Meanwhile, strange scenes were awaiting me when the tour reached New York. I had never been on the East Coast before, and I found the pressure-cooker atmosphere of Manhattan to be overwhelming. Frank had roots in New York; he had spent some of his most fruitful days in Greenwich Village (his spiritual home in some ways, as it had also been the headquarters for his idol, composer Edgard Varèse), and he had many friends who dated back to the Mothers' long run at the Garrick Theater during the '60s. It was a milieu in which I had no place whatsoever.

This was brought very forcibly to my attention when I learned that,

©1995 NIGEY LENNON

Frank's left purple suede shoe. A popular performance routine featured me engaging in simulated erotic acts with it; it later became the 'thong rind' in the song "Andy"

for the first time since I'd been with Frank, I had to cope with competition. The minute we had checked into the Holiday Inn on West 57th Street, the phone rang. Frank was in the living room setting up the stereo he'd rented, so I answered it. There was a pronounced click as the caller hung up. A few minutes later it rang again, and again I answered it. A throaty voice, tinged with laughter, asked to speak to Frank. "Who is this, please?" I asked icily. Right then Frank waltzed in, glared at me, and snatched the phone out of my hand. Not too long afterward, a redheaded avant-garde filmmaker in her mid-20s appeared on the doorstep. She was excruciatingly sophisticated and confident, and Frank was plainly crazy about her. I wasn't; I moped sullenly about until Frank got fed up and called down to the front desk to inquire if they had another room for me. They didn't. I had to sleep on the sofa in the living room; there were two beds in the bedroom, but I couldn't stand being in there, and besides, I hadn't been invited.

I think Frank actually felt a little guilty about the situation, but he was also annoyed that I was cramping his New York lifestyle. What bothered me the most was Miss Moviola's relaxed, comfortable way of dealing with Frank. Watching her made me feel and act a million times klutzier around him. I knew that this universe had existed before me, and I had the feeling it would be continuing long after I was only a few odd magnetic particles on Frank's master tape. As it turned out, I didn't see that much of Frank anyway — he was busy 36 hours a day, introducing the media to *200 Motels*, and engaging in vast quantities of glad-handing, premiere-hosting, interview-giving, and assorted publicity stunts. There was a great deal of interest in the movie because it was the first feature-length film to be shot on video for budgetary reasons and then bumped up to film for general release. Frank made a big point of dragging me to the premiere; he may have just been ensuring that I wouldn't feel left out, but I think he also wanted me to see the film because of its subject — life on the road. Although I didn't feel like going, I dutifully attended the screening, but I was in such a scattered state mentally that the movie failed to leave much of an impression on me.

Back in L.A. a few months later, I saw *200 Motels* again, by myself, in a regular movie theater, with a box of Milk Duds. Although it was easier to concentrate knowing that the writer-composer-director wasn't sitting next to me in the dark, reading my mind, I still found the opus disjointed and formless, and wondered if that was because the whole thing was just over my head conceptually. In actuality, the original script had been much more linear, but the usual cinematic bugaboo, budgetary limitations, had made it impossible to film some crucial sections; the whole thing had been shot on a sound stage in London in a matter of weeks.

Frank was obsessed with the idea of film, but if *200 Motels* was any indication, it appeared that his vision was difficult to translate to the cinematic medium. Maybe to be an effective filmmaker he needed more than sociological archetypes, musical contrasts, and documentation. At any rate, the juxtapositions that worked so well on record and in live performance seemed flat and labored, even a little boring, up on the screen. Luckily, I wasn't a film critic, nor even a film buff, and I never would have expressed my reservations to the *auteur*. I figured it was safer to stick to music and leave the Fellini bit to Frank's Greenwich Village *cineaste* chums. Frank may have envisioned himself as another Bunuel or Eisenstein, but when it came right down to it, in his heart he was still right there with Guitar Slim, and I was there with both of them, eternally prepared to bend some strings. Whatever charms Miss Moviola and her esthetic may have possessed for him, she still couldn't jam all night on the blues with him like I could.

To promote *200 Motels*, Frank arranged a big bash for the band, the media, and a lot of his cronies at Sardi's, the famed show biz watering hole. I wasn't sure if I wanted to go, but I went, and, I'm sorry to say, spent the evening trying to make Frank jealous by flirting shamelessly with the unfortunate band member who had the hots for me. Everybody, meanwhile, was engaging in pretty serious drinking. In my romantic affliction, I too yearned mightily for a slug from the cup that cheers, but I didn't dare order any alcohol. I'd already been "carded" a couple of times during the tour while attempting to obtain a drink in some Podunk Holiday Inn cocktail lounge, and I was concerned that, if I got nailed again here,  in front of all these jaded sophisticates (not to mention *her*), I'd die of mortification. Little did I know that the legal drinking age in New York state was 18, not 21 the way it had been in California.

The next day Frank kept erupting into grumpy little explosions whenever I got within a few feet of him; my cheap ruse the night before had evidently been effective. That night was the second of two sold-out shows at Carnegie Hall, and I had been looking forward to it, if only because I'd be able to tell people I'd appeared at Carnegie Hall (I wasn't planning to mention that my climactic moment was having shaving cream sprayed down the inside of my jeans during an especially rowdy number).

My rival had finally trundled off to her groovy Greenwich abode, and Frank and I had spent the morning consuming room-service bagels and grapefruit juice and listening to a record of an avant-garde work for solo harpsichord by Anthony Newman. Frank thought it was great, while I loudly opined that it was just so much florid *poot*. This apostasy sent him into a fit of harrumphing and fulminating about my youth, *cowboy damage*, and general lack of musical savvy. As he sat on the sofa (with that half sardonic, half pedantic expression and his wild black hair sticking out all over the place, he looked like a prisoner in some 16th-century Florentine dungeon, stuck in there for insisting that the moon orbited the sun), I could see that his feelings were hurt, and I didn't know whether to laugh or to feel sorry for him. I sat down next to him and gave him a hug. He kept on harrumphing, but he also started to stick his hand in my shirt. Then the phone rang again.

Later, I was in the bathroom brushing my teeth, having left him straightening up the living room. Frank, as I'd been learning, wasn't just tidy, he was that most dreaded of domestic monsters, *The Obsessive/Compulsive Organizer* : there had better be a place for everything and everything in its place, because if he went to find that particular little *rentoon-frammin* he was looking for and couldn't, *it was your fault,* and you'd never hear the end of it. I didn't realize why he was like that until he happened to tell an interviewer that when he was growing up his mother had always kept the hardwood floors in their house so highly polished *you could see your reflection in them.* I found this revelation truly frightening.

As I was picking up the bottle of mouthwash, I heard the rattle of flipping pages, then an angry thump. *"Nigey, come here."* That was an order. I'd never heard him sound like that before. I sashayed into the living room and was confronted with the sight of him, mustache fairly bristling with outrage, my journal clutched in his fist. He had seen my little notebook sticking out of my carry-on flight bag, and I guess the temptation to read about himself was just too much for him to resist.

"What are you doing with that?" I asked, feeling the same sort of inarticulate rage I'd experienced when I was twelve and my father, snooping around in my room, had found a mildly smutty poem I'd written, which he claimed disgusted him.

"That's not the point," Frank snapped. "The point is, are you going to run out and sell this stuff to Rolling Stone?"

It was true that I had been keeping detailed notes on the goings-on during the tour. I'd started my journal about the time I discovered "Freak Out!", and as both entertainment and cheap therapy, it had gotten me through the misery of high school, my grandmother's illness and death, and a lot of other things. Like the old Russian fairy tale about Tsar Trajan having goat's ears, my journal was the only place I could set down the whole truth and nothing but the truth as I saw it, without worrying about what anybody was going to think. Frank should have understood that, and in fact he probably would have, if I hadn't been writing about my life on the road with *him*. For some reason he had developed an absolute paranoia about journalists and being written about in general, grimly envisioning elaborate conspiracies by the press to disinform Middle America about

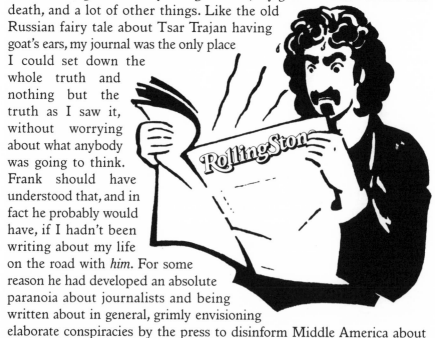

his life's work. It seemed odd to me that he had apparently forgotten how, on several occasions during the tour, I'd pointedly refused to talk to overly inquisitive rock journalists about him and our relationship. He knew that some of my writing on music (though nothing on *him* or *his* music) had been published, and I guess his paranoia had just taken over from there. When his buttons were pushed, Frank, usual rigorously logical, could take solipsism to unheard-of depths.

The whole situation was highly ludicrous; for once, instead of Frank pointing out an inherent absurdity to me, it was the other way around. *The rancid sock was definitely on the other foot, boys and girls.* I tried to explain that my journal was *my* business, and guaranteed to stay that way, but he had gotten all lathered up and self-righteous, and it was no use. No matter what I said, I couldn't convince him that my journal entries weren't going to be the lead exposé in the next issue of Rolling Stone. If I'd been older and wiser, I would have realized that this was his way of venting his multitude of frustrations, but as it was I wound up yelling at him and storming out of the Holiday Inn to lay Gotham to waste. It was the only power I had.

Moments after hailing a cab in front of the Holiday Inn, it occurred to me that I ought to look in my wallet. Ordinarily I carried the necessities of life in an old brown tooled-leather pouch on my belt, but it seemed suspiciously light all of a sudden. One quick, desperate glance inside was enough to confirm my worst fears. Sure enough, I'd stormed out and left my money behind in the suite. By this time the cab had pulled away from the curb and was doing about 15 miles per hour as it entered the thick stream of traffic near Broadway. I let out a howl, seized the door handle, and leaped out. The cabbie was yelling something after me, but I didn't stick around to listen.

Feeling like a cretin, I shambled back up Broadway. There was nothing to do but go up to the Holiday Inn and collect my errant billfold. I went around the corner, walked into the lobby, nodded to the doorman in what I hoped was an imperious manner, and took the elevator up to the 17th floor. The door to the suite was locked. I pulled out my key, unlocked it, and

69

went in. I thought I remembered leaving my wallet on the dresser in the bedroom. As I walked into the living room I noticed that the suite was dark, and imagined Frank going around obsessively making sure all the lights were turned off before he left for Carnegie Hall to putter with the rented sound reinforcement gear. Knowing him, he'd be there scowling, twiddling knobs, and harrumphing until some burly stagehand finally came and dragged him onto the stage for the show.

Still castigating myself for my absent-mindedness, I started to walk into the bedroom. A strong whiff of obviously pricey perfume assailed my nose. There, in the gloom, beneath the sheet on the queen-size bed, was a writhing *entity*, a monster with two backs. I heard muffled moaning, rising in pitch. *Another of Dr. Zurkon's infernal experiments!*

Somehow I found myself in Central Park. I sat down dully on a graffiti-scarred bench near the lake, staring out at the waterfowl and the transients. After some undisclosed and irrelevant period of time Herb Cohen, Frank's manager, happened by and asked why I was sitting there like that.

"You don't want to know," I told him. He agreed; he didn't want to know. He'd been working with Frank for six years, and he'd probably heard it all already.

We strolled around the park with the joggers and the muggers, munching on pretzels and hot chestnuts, while he regaled me with anecdotes about his experiences in the golden era of L.A. coffeehouses, the early '60s. At least he didn't mention Frank. I was glad of that.

When he went off again, I was feeling masochistic, so I decided to take a little trip over to Greenwich Village. It was my first look at it, and I was disgusted to realize that I loved it immediately. I loved the cobblestone streets and the little brass plaques honoring the artistic toilers who had formerly occupied the old, narrow brownstones. In L.A. these charming and admittedly useless monuments would have long ago been razed for parking lots. *This is what Europe's supposed to look like, I guess,* I thought. Then I had a sudden vision of that writhing monster back at the Holiday Inn, and I wished I had a reverse phone directory and a flame-thrower.

In Washington Square Park there were squadrons of panhandlers and flocks of pigeons. I saw one guy who looked like a character in a William Kotzwinkle novel, all malodorous rags and matted hair. He was intently luring unsuspecting birds into an ingenious jury-rigged device constructed from what seemed to be a bunch of coathangers and a small rabbit cage. It looked as though the pigeons were his only source of sustenance; he was so thin he seemed about to blow away. I wondered what he used for bait, but not for very long.

After I'd wandered around some more, I too was starving to death, so I found a deli — and was roundly insulted by the counterman during a semantic imbroglio about what constituted a "plain" cheeseburger. Replete, if a bit mystified by the folkways of Gotham, I came out on the street and glanced at my watch. By now the vile Zurkon would have completed his evil experiment and would be duly ensconced at Carnegie Hall. It was time for me to head back to the Holiday Inn and get some sleep. If he thought I was going to show up for the gig tonight, he was going to be very surprised.

On the way back to the Holiday Inn, the cab passed Carnegie Hall. Dusk was falling fast, but I got a good look at the line-up stretching nearly around the block: desperate mortals hoping to snag tickets for the sold-out show. *Boy, the things I could tell them about their idol Frank Zappa.* Every single last one of them, no matter how fanatic they *had* been, would promptly turn on their heel, march to the nearest League of Decency office, and put in a complaint.

At the Holiday Inn, sure enough, there was nobody in the suite — just a faint vestige of old cigarette smoke and odious cologne in the bedroom. I climbed fully dressed into the unused bed and passed out.

I woke up to the ringing of the phone. Squinting over at the little luminous travel alarm clock on the nightstand, I saw the time was past 1 a.m. I didn't want to answer; it probably wasn't for *me.* But it kept ringing and ringing...Maybe it was Frank, checking up on my whereabouts. Finally I picked it up and mumbled, "Yeah." *Click!*

I couldn't get back to sleep after that, so I went into the living room and chain-smoked the remaining cigarettes in a pack of Camels Frank had left lying around. Along with the disputed Anthony Newman album, there were records by Penderecki, Takemitsu, and "Gatemouth" Brown all stacked neatly against the table. Idly I turned on the FM tuner in the stereo. I flipped past a rock station that was playing "Call Any Vegetable" from the "Live at the Fillmore East" album. I'd never heard it on the radio back in L.A.

It wasn't long before I heard a key in the lock. I slid down to one end of the sofa and crushed out the butt I'd been working on. Frank swept in alone, a fast, fluid swirl of gruesome tweed, and set his guitar down. He came right over to me and, taking off his coat, threw it over the armchair.

"Where were you?" he demanded. When he went into *interrogation mode,* he was as intimidating as hell. Torquemada could have learned all *sorts* of things from Frank. I tried to think of him with his clothes off, hoping to reduce him conceptually to a *ludicrous naked male,* but it did-

71

n't work. Towering over me, with those pitiless eyes drilling right through me, he simply refused to be a character in my movie.

"I decided I'd stay here and get some sleep," I replied. In my stomach that damn cheeseburger was beginning to churn horribly. (Was I about to become the *Spew Queen of West 57th Street*?)

"Well, it was your show. I dedicated it to you. It's going on an album, too."

"Thanks, I guess." Actually, I had to stop and think about that. I'd never figured Frank for the sort of sentimental fool who'd get up — in Carnegie Hall, no less — and make an idiot of himself publicly by *mentioning names* . Hadn't he savagely trashed that whole dedicatory syndrome on "Ruben and the Jets"? I finally heard the tape of the show more than a year later. He'd made a rambling, awkward sort of speech, explaining how he never dedicated shows to anyone, but this was a *special circumstance*, ladies and gentlemen... ***"This show is dedicated to Nigey Lennon, who hitchhiked out here from California." Phew!*** — I'd been getting worried there, but by turning the whole thing into an absurdity at the last minute, he'd just managed to save himself from coming across like the bandleader at the graduation dance at Antelope Valley Joint High School, 1958 (... *"and I'd like to send this slow one out to darlin' Mary Lou from her ever-lovin' Chuy..."*). What he'd really meant, of course, was *"...who rode my face out here from California."*

Turned out there was a reason for this public spectacle, too. He frowned. "We better talk. "

"About what?" I asked, trying to sound indifferent. I knew I couldn't fool Frank, but I'd be damned if *I* was going to let him see how awful I felt.

"Look, I know you're upset," he said, softening a little when he saw my pathetic attempt at coolness. Then he explained that one of the guys in the band had called Mrs. Zappa and told all sorts of lurid tales about our little 'road romance'. Frank knew it was a bald attempt to get me kicked off the tour, but under the circumstances he had no choice. Clearing his throat, he said, "In the morning we're going on to Toronto. I think you should go back to L.A. But" -- he cleared his throat (*stalling for time*, I thought) -- "I've been watching you go through changes over some of this stuff, and I don't want to keep putting you through that. Do you understand?"

"Sure, I understand. You're tired of me and want to get rid of me. You've gotten whatever you wanted, and now it's time for you to move on. Don't sweat it, I'll go. There's no point *my* having any feelings on the subject."

Frank took an inadvertent step backward and almost stumbled. From the look on his face it seemed as if I'd suddenly breached the place where he kept his unbearable memories at bay behind rusted iron doors. Then with an effort he recovered, reached down, and tugged me to my feet, pulling me close to him and holding me there.

"You don't understand. I care about you, but with you here all the time, there's just too much going on. It gets in the way of the things I have to do if I have to be thinking about you and worrying about you all the time."

Jeez, that sounded almost flattering. Was I that much of a distraction?

I should have been angry, but I only felt sadness — sadness unto death. If I could have managed to blurt out the truth, that I loved him and wanted him to treat me like a human being, with dignity and respect — I have no doubt that he would have understood. He'd always wanted to hear that from me. But it was probably too late. Miss Moviola wasn't even part of the problem; the *real* problem was that I had no place in Frank's life, and I never would have. I hadn't wanted to think about this moment, although it had been inevitable from the beginning. Now it was here, and there was nothing I could say to forestall it. I just pressed my face against Frank's shirt and stood there in dumb agony, too hurt and too proud to speak.

Frank held me close to him, his silence eloquent. There was nothing *he* could say, either. Whatever the situation, it wasn't in his character to lie about it or even to soft-pedal it. My thoughts raced painfully — if he wasn't going to say something, maybe I had better. But what? Something? Anything? He'd blasted away my reserve, but the abyss remained, an unbridgable chasm...

I was inundated with scenes from the previous two months: airports, coffee shops, cars, buses... motel rooms: *dark universe, billions and billions...enveloped, exploding, ... that voice: "Maybe we can get one together."* I saw him onstage, masterfully controlling the band... What was that hand signal again — *"Let me know..."*?

I thought of Miss Moviola, of the mutant beast with two backs. That did it: with a blinding flash of light Zurkon's universe imploded, and all of a sudden I was standing in an antiseptic motel living room with an ugly brocade couch and a shag carpet, in the arms of a tall, gangly Italian guy who smelled like coffee and cigarettes and desperately needed a shave.

...Nothing.

There wasn't a fucking thing I could say.

In the morning I rode to JFK on the band bus. I was full of rag-ing emotions — despair, frustration, anger — but mostly I felt an aching sense of loss and injustice, as though I were being unfairly expelled from Utopia. Frank was plainly and visibly exhausted. He'd stayed up with me until almost 5 a.m.; I'd finally fallen asleep with my head on his shoulder, cut off in mid-whimper by a snore. He woke me an hour or so later. Now he was all busi-ness, the road rat on fast forward. He had his suitcases and gear waiting by the door, and in very few words he told me to get packed; the bus was wait-ing downstairs, and everyone but us was on it.

For the first time since I'd joined the tour, we didn't sit together; look-ing like death warmed over, he deliberately took a seat by himself in the back of the bus. Miss Moviola had given him a parting gift, a smutty novel by Aleister Crowley. *How very appropriate.* I peeked back at him. He was pretending to read it, but he wasn't turning the pages very fast.

At the airport I had to find a flight to LAX; I hadn't had time to make a reservation by phone. At least I had plenty of dough — Frank had settled up with me before leaving that morning, in cash. (I couldn't help won-dering where those brand new hundreds and fifties came from. As I stuck the 'wad' in my wallet, it all seemed slightly sleazy to me, although the explana-tion wasn't anything more sinister than the fact that Frank, knowing I did-n't have a checking account, had gotten the cash for me from Herbie or Dick.)

Frank and his band of merry men were bound for the international flight section. As they headed off in that direction, some of the guys were spiritedly bellowing a little ditty, full of charming obscenities about the tits and ass and cheap thrills to be found just around the bend. It sounded patho-logically cheerful in that dismal terminal, and there were gloomy glares from the gray commuters waiting for their grim flights to their bleak destinations in the freezing North.

I had written a little farewell note to Frank, and I walked over and handed it to him. It said:

F.Z. —

I know you don't believe in love. Well, then, take mine and use it for vacuum cleaner bags or something.

— N.L.

74

He tucked it into the back of the book, but didn't seem about to actually read it, at least not in front of me. I knew better than to expect anything as conventional as "Goodbye, it's been nice knowing you" from him; he'd bid me farewell in front of a sold-out house in Carnegie Hall last night, and then he'd kicked out my ass in private — what more did I want? Skywriting? What a fucking masochist I was!

I forced myself not to hesitate; without further ado I turned and began to trudge resolutely toward the domestic flight counters. I had to physically struggle not to turn around and take one last look at him, but I managed to get around the corner without doing it.

It was just my accursed luck that there were no nonstops available to LAX that day; the only flight out of there before midnight required a transfer at O'Hare in Chicago. When I boarded the plane for the first leg of the flight, I felt like I was being nailed into my coffin. The minute I was in my seat I accosted the stewardess and demanded a double dry

vodka martini. She hesitated, and I groaned inwardly, *Oh shit, what a time for me to get carded again.* Then, seeing my haggard face, she quietly went back to the galley and brought out two plastic cups full of clear liquid, a twist of lemon dangling over each rim. "On the house, sweetie," she said simply. A saint.

I took a deep, soul-saving quaff, opened my carry-on bag, and looked around inside it for something to keep me from going crazy. And what were the first objects therefrom to catch my eye? Frank's sock —

The Sock, my fetish totem — and my fucking *journal.* I heard Guitar Slim moaning, "You're all packed up and ready to leave me, baby, and the good Lord knows I'm about to die...but just before you leave me, please give me something to remember you by..."

"I hate you, Frank Zappa," I growled savagely into the first martini. It was almost gone. I drained it and seized the other with a hand that should have been covered in coarse black hair.

My seatmate, a motherly Midwestern sort of lady, who was sitting next to the window, turned and stared at me as if she'd just seen me take off my shirt and reveal a snarling werewolf tattooed across my tits in flaming red. ꞴꝊꝎꞰ ꞰꝊ ꝆꝊꟍꝎ.

Stuck in the bottom of my bag I found the copy of "Slaughterhouse Five" I'd bought at some airport gift shop several weeks ago but had been too *otherwise occupied* to find time to read. Well, there was *plenty* of time now. Yes, I was *choking* on the stuff. Didn't it just feel *great,* ladies and gentlemen?

This was going to be *twelve hours in hell* . I downed the last martini in a single horrible gullop, belched atavistically, and stuck out my *poot-stomper* to trip the stewardess as she came up the aisle wheeling the drink cart. From some recess of the damp, echoing grottoes in my mind I heard a strangled half-growl, half-groan, the sound of incisors quietly, efficiently rending epidermis as *Werewolves Ripped My Flesh* ...

By the way, I've never been back to New York since then.

CHAPTER 7

My Continuing Education

Back in L.A. again, and things were, with due apologies to Fats Waller, slightly less than wonderful. I had been gone for more than two months, and my father had been forced to replace me in the shipping department. My mother, meanwhile, had appointed herself a media vigilante vs. *The Zappa Threat* . She had seen Frank being interviewed on the Johnny Carson Show (taped while we were in New York) and determined that he was a]*a degenerate*; b] *a drug addict*; c] *suffering from some acute and nameless disease not classifiable by medical science, but still eminently communicable*; and/or d] *Sicilian,* and therefore automatically *a card-carrying member of the Cosa Nostra.* She was batting .500 on item d] and more or less in the ballpark with item a], but I was sorry she was so set against him. I wished there was some way she could understand how, despite the contradictory nature of our relationship, he had sometimes bordered on being the best mother I'd ever had.

Since I had no job, I therefore enrolled on probationary status at El Camino College, hoping I could pull down a student loan. (They were giving them out with a pretty free hand in those days.) I had a little trouble determining my major, since I was only allowed to take a limited number of courses until I had *proved myself worthy of higher education.* My first love was music, of course, but I had always had a fascination with science and language as well. If I learned, say, German, I'd at least be able to read the writing on the men's room walls in Berlin. The way I was feeling, I might be able to do that *soon* — in fact I'd already

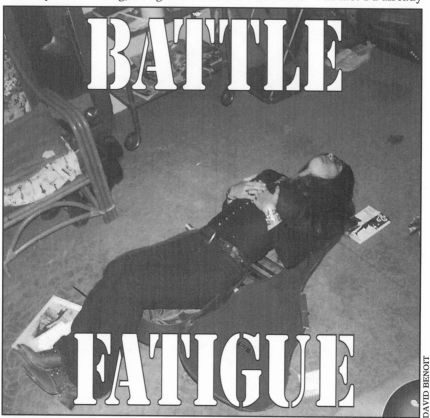

Battle fatigue: My sometime musical accomplice David Benoit took this snapshot of me pretending to be dead in my empty guitar case a couple of days after I got back from the tour

checked with the French Foreign Legion about signing on, but unfortunately they didn't accept female recruits.)

In the end I decided to go with a truly inspired program, majoring in music and minoring in General Semantics. I dropped out of premed, my third choice, before a mysterious explosion in the chem lab had a chance to land me on the dean's list. To this day I retain a great fondness for nitroglycerine and potassium permanganate — otherwise I might be a brain surgeon, or worse.

It turned out to be a small world — Wally Bauer, my Music Theory and Composition I professor, said he knew Frank. He claimed Frank had commissioned him to orchestrate the composition "Igor's

Boogie" (a band version of which appeared on Frank's "Burnt Weeny Sandwich" album) in the style of Stravinsky. I wasn't entirely convinced about the verity thereof, but I liked Mr. Bauer's teaching style. He had a snappy bunch of mnemonic devices — for instance, he described the notation of the two notes constituting a minor-second interval as resembling *"a cat's balls"*.

In my Keyboard course, we had to specialize in a particular instrument. Everybody chose the piano because most of the students had pianos at home to practice on. I didn't, so I signed up for pipe organ. There was a brand new three-rank pipe organ in a soundproof booth at the back of the rehearsal bunker. You had to start it with an ignition key, like a car; the key fired up an electric motor which drove the bellows that pumped the air through the pipes, thereby using the miracles of modern science to eliminate the troublesome serf that had been required to hand-pump the bellows back in the *Good Old Days*. Mrs. Hardester was the organ mistress (she also directed the *a cappella* choir, which I sang tenor in), and I imagine she'll never forget the day when she came running back to the organ cubicle, terrified that we were experiencing the seismic Armageddon the pundits had been predicting. I had discovered *the thrill of holding down the two very lowest adjacent pedals, B natural and C natural, at the same time.* There's something soul-satisfying about the low pedal notes on a pipe organ anyway, but in this case the resulting interference tone was causing such a vibration that every window and doorframe in the bunker was threatening to disintegrate. A crack had actually developed in the heavy plate glass of the window that isolated the pipe organ area from the rest of the practice rooms. I guess they replaced the window eventually; I was never invited back there, for some reason, so I never found out.

My favorite class, though, was Conducting. As Frank had discovered, I couldn't sight read music worth a damn, but being the victim of a pathologically retentive memory, I *could* memorize whole scores easily. Toscanini probably wasn't rolling over in his grave with anxiety, though, because when the buffer in my resident memory got too full, I experienced *data-reduction amnesia* and started to transpose previously memorized scores on top of the current one. This caused a spectacular moment when I was being tested on a movement of Mahler's *Song of the Earth*. I suddenly drew a total blank and thought it was something out of the Ring

Cycle. (Late 19th-century repertory all sounded pretty similar to me anyway.) I started feverishly cueing entrances that could never exist in *any* piece, and flipping the pages of the master score after maybe twenty seconds per page. To draw attention away from the fact that I was rapidly approaching pan-tonal, polyrhythmic *meltdown,* I began flailing around with the baton like I was fending off an attack of bats. The students in the orchestra probably thought somebody had slipped LSD into the drinking fountain. It was a hell of a performance, but I still got a D. After that Mr. Hamilton suggested I leave the baton on his desk and conduct *with my bare hands.* "It'll be safer that way," he pleaded.

It wasn't long before the pleasures and challenges of higher education, while engrossing, began to be sabotaged by increasingly frequent lapses of judgment regarding *"that ugly Italian boyfriend of yours"* (my mother's description). As time went by and I gradually forgot how bad I'd felt that last night on West 57th Street, I stopped being furious and angry, and started thinking about my Gibson 335. I'd left it with Frank because by the time he'd finished fooling with it I could barely play it, but I still wanted it back. From Canada, the tour had continued on to Europe, with a return date scheduled for late December. If I didn't hear from our boy when he got back to L.A., maybe I'd just have to head up to Laurel Canyon and repossess my property.

One Saturday night when I'd been back from the tour for almost two months, I got called to fill in for the regular guitar player at a bar gig in El Porto. I'd gone to Our Lady of Guac with the guys in the band; they'd been working this particular two-niter at this particular watering hole for a long while. I was far from their first call, but that weekend every other guitar player who lived in the South Bay was out of town — I think there was a big outdoor rock festival down near San Diego someplace: *Lee Michaels!* I didn't look forward to jamming on "Ain't No Sunshine" and "Satin Doll," not after my recent triumph with the fanfare from *Agon,* but better to earn $20 honestly than spend another night sitting in my miserable little room at my folks' house, fetishing that *increasingly biologically active* sock and blubbering.

I never subjected my L5 to bar gigs, so tonight I had a bor-rowed Stratocaster which belonged to some idiot guy I barely knew. He lived in Portuguese Bend and didn't even *play* the guitar, but he was loan-ing it to me in the hopes he could weasel an *oral rental payment* out of me. *Jeezuz Kee-reist!!* I was feeling positively truculent; maybe I'd whip out the 3/8 Sears Craftsman socket I used as a slide when I played coun-try and blues material, and give him some *oral payment* all right — but not quite the way he was hoping, the swine.

I pulled up a bar stool in front of the pathetic old Fender Champ the joint used as its house amp. Some drunk had kicked a big hole in the speaker grille, back in 1962 or so. I plugged in and started to tune, trying to ignore the obviously well- lubricated, fortyish fellow who had dragged his stool up next to mine and was asking dumb, opening-gam-bit type questions. *"Gee, how long have you been a musician? You live around here?"* As late as I was, I was still the first of the musicians to show up at the gig. Everything here ran on *South Bay Time,* which was sort of like bar time; when you combined these two *temporal concepts,* South Bay Time and bar time, you wound up in the *Manana Triangle,* wasting away in Harvey Wallbangerville, like most of the locals did. I definitely could have used a beer myself at the moment, but the owner was too cheap (or too wise) to let the musicians run up a tab.

There was an enormous TV set over the bar. Usually it was tuned to The Game, but tonight the 10 o'clock news was on instead. I was try-ing to decide whether I had time to put on new strings — these were the ones that had originally come with the Strat, back in 1959 or thereabouts — when I perked up my ears. Damn, I really *was* obsessing too much over Frank — I'd have sworn I just heard his name mentioned on the 10 o'clock news. I looked up, and there on the vast screen was a watery-looking picture of Frank, a file photo taken about a year ago. Seeing his face, that smile that reminded me of — well, of things I had no business think-ing about in this hellhole of a bar — my heart both sank and leaped. *I wonder what they're saying about him...* He couldn't have finally won a Grammy, could he?

I tried to make out over all the dismal bar noise what the TV newscaster was saying. Something about London. Yep, according to my calculations, the band would be in London now. (I'd been following the itinerary, marking off the stops. L.A., the end of the tour, was getting clos-er all the time; I was beginning to rehearse my guitar-repo strategy with mounting feverishness.) Then I nearly fell off my bar stool. The news-caster was saying something about Frank being in the *hospital* — I could just barely make out the words *concussion,* and *broken leg.* And the worst of all — **serious condition** ! Oh Lord, *please* make this just a fucking nightmare. I'll wake up and it'll be Monday morning and I'll have fall-en asleep listening to my crappy cassette tapes of the tour on head-phones again and missed my pipe organ class. This doesn't make any sense, hearing on the news that Frank's been injured in London. What the fuck had happened to put him in the hospital with all those *mondo* injuries a-go-go??

I had a phone number in Sherman Oaks for Ruth Underwood, the wife of Ian Underwood, the band's keyboard player and a longtime Zappa sideman. We had struck up a superficial sort of friendship dur-ing the tour, and she'd invited me to stop by and visit. She hadn't been on the whole tour, and I thought I remembered her saying that she'd be back in L.A. by now.

I made some brusque, incoherent excuses to the pub owner, stuck the Strat back in its case, and jumped ship. I still didn't have a car, but my parents' house was only two miles south of El Porto. At the curb I stuck out my thumb — this was no fucking time to walk, and the buses had stopped running. A station wagon full of stoned blonde guys in their teens and early 20s stopped right away when they saw I was carry-ing a guitar. They offered me a joint while we were poking along on Highland Avenue, but I demurred. "It's *sensi,*" the driver said with faint censure, looking away from the road to wave the reeking spliff in my face. "The primoest of the primo."

"I don't smoke," I said wearily, "but thanks."

And then I pulled out my pack of Winstons, said a silent and des-perate prayer for *that ugly Italian boyfriend of mine,* and lit up.

It was late, but fortunately Ruth was home and still awake, and she was full of details, some of them alarming. Frank had been punched hard, then pushed off the stage and into the orchestra pit by some psy-cho during the encore at the Rainbow Theater in London. The lunatic claimed his girlfriend had a crush on Frank. He also complained to the press that he hadn't gotten his money's worth. Talk about your *consumer complaints* ... He had been hauled off to the Bridewell, or wherever it was they took felons and Labor MP's.

"I wonder if Jack the Ripper's girlfriend was a redhead," I mused, my knee jerking.

Frank was — Ruth continued breathlessly — lying in the hos-

pital in London with a severe concussion, a shattered leg, a bunch of smashed-up ribs, and maybe a broken neck. Right now his future looked cloudy; maybe he'd walk again, play the guitar again...maybe not; his arm was paralyzed, and it was too early to tell.

I thanked her and hung up. It's got to be the worst feeling in the world to know something dreadful is going on someplace thousands of miles away and you can't do a single thing about it. I had no money to grab a flight to London and no idea what use I'd be to Frank even if I could somehow get there. I visualized myself valiantly breaking down the hospital door and racing to Frank's bedside...where I'd probably encounter three or four weeping redheads, no doubt. (As it turned out, my old ex-roommate Miss Moviola *was* there, along with another young lady, probably *also* a redhead. Frank's wife had found them both keeping a bleary round-the-clock watch over the patient when she'd caught the first available red-eye and rushed straight to the intensive care ward to see him. Luckily for Frank, he was unconscious, or he probably would have been *dead. **What a guy... .***)

It occurred to me that Frank's attacker, while a nut case, was probably just a more *active* individual than his some of his equally wacked-out fellow audience members who'd never tried to injure their hero. Because of its 'outsider' subtext, it was only natural that Frank's music attracted losers and loners of all stripes. A fair number of these people didn't know and probably couldn't care less that their icon actually knew when to hang up his bizarreness and go home; they were probably all confusing the medium with the messsage to some extent. Frank did stress responsibility as well as the more 'outside' aspects of his personality, but when you were high on that sort of rush, it was easy to bypass *the other stuff* entirely. In no way had Frank deserved what happened to him, but from another angle, he had written the script for the movie. I wondered if he was lying in his hospital bed trying not to think about that.

Ruth continued to supply me with medical bulletins every couple of days. The running commentary rather resembled a boxing match: "He's up. He's down. They say he may not play the guitar ever again...No, he's getting feeling back in his hand. He's up...The leg is in a cast. Hmm — it's broken in a weird place and won't set right. They suggested it needed to be broken again and reset, and he cheerfully told them to fuck themselves. He's down again..."

I knew what some of those injuries were like. I'd broken this and that myself, in my rodeo days, and I figured at least Frank would at least be pumped full of morphine, anyway. Turned out he wasn't. He suffered through his recovery essentially without painkillers because he had a head injury, and the doctors didn't want to run the risk of causing brain damage, or spinal cord problems, or malpractice suits, or some such idiocy.

I got hold of the phone number of the clinic where Frank was supposed to be stuck for the next few weeks. It was in Harley Street, where upper class Londoners went to 'enjoy poor health'. I waited until it was about 8 in the morning there and called. The phone had that funny double Euro-ring to it: *Bzzt-bzzt. Bzzt-bzzt.* When the clinic switchboard finally picked up and I said I was calling long distance for Frank Zappa, the lady who answered chuckled like she'd heard that one before. She asked for my name, and I hesitated. "Uh — I'm a member of his band," I said. There was a pause, and a bunch of clicking on the line, and finally a voice I'd heard before, indirectly, a low alto, against a trans-Atlantic background of white noise. "Hello, who is this?" I declined to state, hung up, and didn't call again. I felt cowardly, but it somehow didn't seem like a very good idea.

Frank finally returned home a month later in a wheelchair, with a cast up to his hip. In the hospital, he'd been visited by a deputation of the band members. They had asked how long his recovery was likely to take, and when they realized they might have to go a while without paying work, they bailed. He had been intending to release an album of material from the tour, but since the band was broken up for good, he had evidently decided to move on to new territory and put the past behind him.

I debated whether I should pay a little sympathy call to *Chez Zappa*, the Laurel Canyon rancho, and give Frank a nice bouquet of pansies to try and cheer him up. He definitely needed cheering — not only had he been injured and deserted, but a couple of weeks before his accident, a fire at the Montreux Casino had destroyed all of the band's equipment. I wondered if the fire had spared my Gibson, and I decided to go ask Frank what had happened to it.

One afternoon I purloined my parents' new Mazda station wagon (the same recalled rotary engine model that developed a sticky throttle mechanism after 50,000 miles, causing a number of unwitting Mazda owners to *dance themselves to death*) and drove to Hollywood. I turned up Laurel Canyon Boulevard and picked my way through the rush hour traffic (back in those days it hardly amounted to a trickle) until I got to the top of the incline. I turned onto Frank's street and pulled up in a little cul-de-sac across from his house.

Nothing looked any different. The big Mercedes was still in the driveway. The security fence was as stout and impenetrable as ever. I rolled down my window and listened. Nothing. Just an endless-loop version of John Cage's *4'33"* — silence. No amazing guitar chords. I hesitated, then quietly got out and crossed the street. Next to the gate stood a big metal U.S. Postmaster-Approved mailbox on a post. I opened it slowly so the door wouldn't squeak. Inside was a thick pile of envelopes, little parcels, and magazines, probably two or three days' worth of mail. On top was a postcard with an air mail stamp. I didn't mean to snoop, but I couldn't help noticing that it was signed, "Miss you! When are you comming *(sic)* back? Much love — Greta." Now just why was I receiving this psychic transmission that Greta might possibly have...

...red hair?

There went my damn knee again. I stuffed my big bouquet of purple flowers, tied together with a purple sock, into the mailbox orifice. Then I shut the mailbox door, got back in the car, and drove away.

CHAPTER 8

The Young Person's Guide to Explosives

T hings began to get very strained at my parents'. I couldn't really blame them; here I was, looking down the barrel of my 18th birthday, and I was still no closer to charting a sensible course in the straits of Life than I ever had been. I had sold a couple more music reviews to local publications, picked up an odd music-copying job or two, played an actual paying gig leading a band opening for Dave Mason (*remember him?*) at an arena concert in Long Beach (psychedelic blues jams in E and A), and quietly bowed out of El Camino. When the student loan administration saw my parents' tax return, they had nixed my application for a loan. I didn't have the energy to work full time *and* go to classes, so I bid a reluctant farewell to a potentially fulfilling career as an unemployed music professor making ends meet as a low-paid, part-time teaching assistant in General Semantics with a full-time job as a cocktail waitress in the Marina.

I was on the verge of being officially evicted from the family domicile, and had been making tentative, grovelsome approaches to various friends about sleeping on their floors and couches, when one night around 10 p.m., the phone rang. My mother, a spectacular panorama in her ratty flannel nightgown and green face cream, grumbled, "Your inconsiderate friends, as usual?" I snatched up the receiver. "Hello," I said testily.

"*Hey...*" The voice was much quieter than it should have been, and sounded muffled and lower in pitch than I remembered.

I spluttered, regained a semblance of composure, managed to stammer out a greeting of sorts, and asked him how he was doing. I did it in on auto pilot in a fog, my heart thumping so loudly I suspected he could hear it on his end of the phone.

"I'm awreet," he said simply. "Listen, we just got the insurance settlement on Montreux. During the fire, your guitar was in the anvil case backstage with a bunch of other equipment we had- n't been using lately, and when that part of the building went, everything in there all got sort of scorched together. All Dick could find of it afterward was the tailpiece and one of the melt- ed tuners. They figure blue book on it is four hundred. I think that's kind of a hose job, but hey, what you gonna do? It's the American Way...You want to pick it up at the office, or do you want it mailed to you?"

"Uh, well....is there any way I can get it in cash?" Since I had nothing to put in it, I still didn't have a checking account. Four hun- dred dollars was a fortune to me; I could live for six months on it. Besides, the Gibson had only cost me $125 originally.

On the other end of the line I could hear the faint click of a lighter and the old familiar exhalation of smoke. Suddenly all I wanted was to put my hand on him, on his face or arm or the top of one of his thighs, the skinny devil...anywhere, it didn't matter. I wanted to touch him and make sure he was still there and still felt the same.

"I could get the cash if you can wait a couple days. We're rehears- ing Thursday — you can pick it up then."

"OK, that'll be great. Where's the rehearsal?"

"It's at 150 North La Brea, at one o'clock."

I scribbled down the address on a matchbook. "Well — see you then."

"Awreet." What was with all this "awreet" bizness, anyway? Was he hanging around these days with a bunch of doofuses in berets and goatees, or what? It made him sound like he was wearing a zoot suit, for Chrissakes.

On Thursday I 'liberated' the Mazda and roared toward Hollywood, blasting one of my clandestinely-recorded tour tapes on the car cassette as I went careening along the eastbound Santa Monica Freeway. Old ugly, dull monochrome life had suddenly exploded into Technicolor 3-D again, and the only fitting soundtrack was *Little Carl the Penguin being flung through the flaming hoop!...* "of course we'll play *Petrouchka* !"

I was rather surprised by the abject nondescriptness of 150 North La Brea. The two-storefront-wide, windowless rehearsal facility, on the east side of the street, north of Wilshire Boulevard, was wedged between a synagogue ladies' auxiliary second-hand shop and a liquor store. From the sidewalk, it could have been anything — a temple of Gnosticism or a sweatshop, take your pick. On the other side of La Brea was an Orthodox Jewish synagogue and religious school. There was a furniture upholsterer up the block, and a Cadillac dealer on the corner. Not a very likely place to go looking for a thrill, I mused as I parked the Mazda right out front and fruitlessly probed my person for parking change.

After half an hour or so, musicians began pulling up in the tiny (two spaces) parking area in the rear. They'd unload their gear from their cars, drag it into the rehearsal hall through the rear door, then rush back out to move their cars. There were lots of musicians — this seemed to be an enormous band. Dozens of guys were hauling in what looked like saxes and brass instruments, including a French horn, a euphonium, and a tuba, and there was one woman schlepping a *bassoon case.* For a second I wondered if I'd gotten the address wrong and was about to crash a Philharmonic rehearsal.

Then I saw one of the guys from the road band unloading his equipment. He acknowledged me with a sociable leer and we exchanged a few pleasantries. When he reached into an anvil case for some hardware, I spotted a fading Polaroid photo that had been taken at one of the shows on the tour — Frank, with a dementedly didactic expression, holding the microphone toward me while I used it to demonstrate *obscure Tibetan marital arts* to the audience. Seeing it conjured up a flood — actually a puddle — of memories.

When the cars started to pile up more than two or three deep in the back, the musicians had to resort to the curb out front, which was a No Stopping zone, and bring their equipment in the front way. The problem was the enterprising meter maid lurking just out of sight, waiting for each hapless blower or strummer to stumble into her web. I never saw so many parking tickets handed out in such a short time. If it had been Las Vegas instead of Los Angeles, that meter maid would have probably been the next mayor or something.

Apprehensively, I drifted in through the back door, stood toward the rear, out of harm's way, and "sussed it out". It was plain where Frank had acquired his "awreet" jive from — the small room was crammed full of *jazz-looking guys* in metal chairs — guys with goatees, guys in berets, guys sucking on their reeds, blowing saliva out of their spit valves, and sliding their pistons back and forth. It looked like he'd conducted his auditions at the Old Beboppers' Home.

The noise level was worse than earsplitting. Suddenly, without warning, I felt almost dizzy, and my ears began to ring. *"Hey!"* Virtually compelled to turn around, I felt rather than saw Frank looking at me from across the room, and I slowly walked over to him.

He was sitting awkwardly, his left leg stuck out stiffly and painfully. The minute I got up close to him I could feel that his energy level was low. Everything about him seemed out of synch, stunned, diminished. As he looked up at me, I saw that there were deep, blue-black shadows under his eyes, and his expression radiated a sort of cosmic incredulity. He was still trying to come to terms with a world where somebody could *do* that to him; the brutal fact of *assault,* of violation, had left him devastated and bewildered.

Not entirely voluntarily, I half knelt down and put my arms around him. He hugged me back, even hung on to me for a moment, and suddenly I caught a flash of his old energy again. With a wicked grin he thrust forward his broken leg, showing me that it was held together with a mean-looking steel brace and pins, and the foot encased in a prosthetic shoe. "How's *that* for a shoe?" he smirked — a private joke which brought back all-too-vivid memories of the tour. "Thank you for the floral tribute," he added, indicating his uninjured right foot, which was shod in a more conventional manner. He was wearing the purple sock I'd wrapped around his bouquet.

He leaned over slowly and opened his briefcase, took out a business-size envelope, and handed it over to me. "It's all there, but if you wanna count it, go ahead." I unstuck the flap and drew out another 'wad' — four stiff, new-smelling C-notes — and tucked them into my wallet.

Meanwhile, some of the musicians were eyeing us curiously. Frank promptly added to their prurient interest. "I have here something that oughta curl up *your* toes a little bit," he told me, and went groping in the briefcase amidst the music paper and finished charts. "Aha!" he declared, and triumphantly hauled out *a lollipop in the shape of a bare foot.* It had a little card hanging off it with a poem about *sucking on toes* and *feet taking their licks.* Jeez, I hoped I wasn't blushing in front of all these jaded jazzbos; my face was burning. Frank presented this demented trophy to me with a flourish and a little bow — not an easy gesture for somebody who basically can't move from the waist down. Maybe you couldn't murder a case-hardened absurdist that easily after all.

I thanked him, squatted down in front of him, and read the card out loud. He guffawed with me, raised that old eyebrow, and — *here we go again, boys and girls, from the top: one, two, three.* What could he still want with me, after all we'd been through? Shit — what was left? Worse, why had my own judgment and willpower just fizzled out and delivered me right back into his clutches without even a whimper of doubt or warning, when I knew that the minute I started seeing him again there was *no way* I could stand back on the sidelines and maintain my cool? Didn't I  remember all the pain and suffering I'd been undergoing these last few months? Did I, *hell* — at that precise moment, when I should have been heading straight home, do not pass Go, do not forget your four hundred dollars — can you guess what I was thinking?

*Oh gosh, I wonder if his **wedding tackle** was affected by the accident!* (It wasn't.)

He showed me the music he'd been writing for this new group. It was fully scored, not merely chord charts to songs but full-blown chamber orchestra parts, horn transpositions and all.

"When did you write these?" I wanted to know.

"I finished this one this morning," he said, rolling his eyes heavenward. "I haven't had a chance to copy the parts yet."

This struck me as heroic work, under the circumstances. He would have earned the right, after nearly being killed by some lunatic, just to lie around and groan, but instead he'd forced himself back to work, had composed this mutant chamber music, and now was going to forge ahead and play it. That put a new spin on the word "character," I reflected.

I took a seat near him so I could peer over his shoulder at the scores. As usual, he was being very serious about the appurtenances of the job — the completed parts had all been ozalid-reproduced at Cameo Music, and were tucked inside an imposing black folder with THE GRAND WAZOO, the name of the group, on the front in gold lettering. Frank had even obtained a regulation baton. It looked like he was about to break it in, although in my experience, I had never heard of anybody but me who had actually worn one out.

When all the musicians were warmed up, Frank (seated by necessity, but stalwartly leading nonetheless raised an authoritative hand and asked them to play an A. Some of the players raised wry eyebrows, but *hey, they were drawing scale...* so out it came, that familiar 440 pitch in all those different timbres. It sounded remarkably like an orchestra. I got the goosepimply feeling I'd first experienced as a four-year-old when my parents had taken me to a Leonard Bernstein "Young People's Guide to the Orchestra" concert at the Hollywood Bowl; when the entire massed strings, woodwinds, brass, and percussion had frenziedly thrown themselves into a *huge writhing pile* on the first *triple forte* section in Stravinsky's *Firebird*, I had gotten up and stood there frozen, with my eyes and tongue hanging out, until my mortified mother finally dragged me back to my seat. An orchestra was, I'd just realized in my kiddie way, a wonderfully dangerous machine. **You could blow things to kingdom come with it.**

Frank seemed satisfied that the parts of *his* machine were all in working order, so he raised his baton, counted off a couple of bars for nothing, gave the downbeat, and there it was: that old feeling of exhilarated hyper-consciousness I remembered so well. I looked down at the master score he was conducting from. It was all right there on paper in the form of all those familiar little dots and crossbars, no mystery about it, so how could it make me I feel like every barricade in my mind had just been exploded clear into the Great Beyond? I glanced toward the musicians, all huffing and puffing and moving the air molecules around like longshoremen. They were too busy trying to nail the pesky notes and tricky rhythms to care about metaphysics. *This was really interesting.* I was going to have to ask Frank some very deep questions sooner or later.

CHAPTER 9

Home, Home and Deranged

I began spending every waking hour at Grand Wazoo rehearsals. I felt that I had vast lessons to learn; all I wanted to do was stand next to Frank, reading over his shoulder while he conducted or played his guitar, and watching how the score was transformed from notes on paper into audio by the musicians. Until now my exposure to the creation and production of orchestral music had been minimal; I knew from my embryonic studies that music was written by composers in the form of notes on paper, and that when the notes were played by musicians, they were transformed into *very dense air* , but this was my first opportunity to watch the whole process from little dots-on-paper all the way through audible molecules.

After a few rehearsals I realized that at every rehearsal there was an extra chair placed next to Frank's conducting stand. Never too fast on the uptake, it finally occurred to me that it was *my* chair. No one else ever sat in it; it was my place in the band. (I *had* thought about asking Frank if I could audition for the group, either on guitar or keyboards, but this new material was far more demanding than the stuff the road band had been playing. It required orchestral level sight-reading skills, for one thing. Knowing I'd never pass the audition, now or later, I finally settled into my chair and forced myself to quit being so obsessed with the impossible. I didn't want to wind up like *Frank* , did I??)

Frank was completely focused on the business at hand: composing music for this particular group, and hearing them play it. I watched him going through the process, which seemed much more *formal* than all the shenanigans associated with road life, and wondered how he reconciled these distinctly different aspects of whatever it was he did. Naturally my motivations for being at rehearsals weren't entirely pure; I was curious whether our business might resume at the old stand, of course. A few rehearsals passed without occurrence; then one afternoon Frank brought in a new piece, entitled "RDNZL". I helped him pass out all the parts and sat back to listen while he put the players through their paces. Most of the Grand Wazoo material was like riding the Cyclone Racer coaster at the Long Beach Pike — full of turns and twists and dynamics and thrilling climaxes. But the instant I heard the first statement in "RDNZL" — arranged for the horns, rhythm section, and percussion in massed unison, and tossed off so fast I could only catch half the notes and about a quarter of the inner rhythms — as played by that incarnation of musicians, in the distinctly non-climate-controlled Temple of Wazoodom on a fiercely smoggy afternoon, with traffic groaning and screeching past outside on La Brea, I was so overwhelmed by the experience that I wanted to lie down on the floor.

Out of a misplaced sense of decorum, I stayed in my seat, but I looked over at Frank, who was only a few feet away from me. He was awkwardly standing up, conducting from the master score on his music stand. Generally, when he introduced the group to a new piece, he ran all the way through it once without stopping, clinkers and breakdowns and all, both to give the musicians an idea of the shape of the composition and to hear for himself how it had turned out. The players were nearly all 'first call' pros from orchestral and studio backgrounds, and they were more than capable of a clean reading the first time through. Today they happened to be flawless. I caught Frank's eye; he looked back at me for a second and saw that I was (as he observed later) *"about to reach nirvana, or apoplexy, or something"*, and he smiled at me, that old familiar *rancid socks & hemiolas* smile I remembered from the road when he'd really liked something I'd just done. As he cued a bass clarinet entrance, I began to have the strange sensation that he was employing the group the way he'd formerly utilized some of those *other* random objects, *to get me off.* When he looked at me again with an expression of utter amusement and *doubled the already inhuman tempo* , it was obvious what he was up to. I'm sure the musicians were entirely oblivious to the situation; if they'd known what was going on, they'd probably have demanded triple performance scale. To this day "RDNZL" remains my single favorite Frank Zappa composition. My only regret was that the whole performance wasn't somehow recordable for posterity.

Due to my perfect attendance record at the rehearsals, it wasn't long before I was nearly as familiar with the music as Frank was, and since I usually showed up at rehearsals about the same time as he did, and he was still pretty immobilized, he started handing me his briefcase and letting me pass out the parts. I felt a bit embarrassed because I was so obviously spending my entire life at those rehearsals, and I was glad to be able to earn my keep any way I could. Frank, of course, was well aware of my embarrassment and was trying to make me feel a little less ridiculous while at the same time making his life easier. Maybe he was reminded of his own days of adolescent orchestral klutziness. I wanted to tell him how much I appreciated being able to hear this stuff on a firsthand basis, how from my point of view it was the equivalent of, say, him being able to stand at Varèse's elbow and watch him working on "Desérts" or something. But once or twice, when the chance to say something presented itself, I'd open my mouth and nothing would come out. It wasn't the first time.

My parents finally reached the end of their respective ropes with me. One night my father came home from work and sat down in his easy chair with a grim look on his face. He and my mother had obviously been conferring. I didn't wait for the verdict; I went upstairs, packed all of my clothes in an old suitcase and some brown paper bags, then went down and stuck the stuff in the trunk of my 1962 Ford Fairlane, which I'd recently bought with $150 of the insurance check. Next I got my guitar, amp, and music supplies, and loaded them into the back seat. Finally I came back into the house, went into the den, and told my parents goodbye. My mother turned away without speaking. My father looked as if there was something on his mind, but if there was, he didn't say it. I walked out, feeling like the world was ending but not caring if it did because it was such a shitty place.

I spent the night at a friend's, and the next day dragged into the Temple of the Grand Wazoo feeling disembodied and unreal. Frank kept a watchful eye on me during the rehearsal, and at the end, when I brought back all the parts as usual, he put his hand on my shoulder and observed, "You look like you definitely need to *'feature your hurt.'*"

I told him how I'd been kicked out of my folks' house, not explaining that it was because I was too busy attending Wazoo U to get a job — or a life, for that matter.

Frank grimaced and shook his head as if he was trying to clear out a few unpleasant memories of his own. "Well," he said, adopting the motherly/fatherly stance he had always used when lecturing me on the facts o' life, "maybe we can find you a cubbyhole."

Puzzled, I asked him where. He said that if I'd give him my solemn promise to leave him alone when he was working, I could stay at his place until I found permanent lodgings elsewhere. There was a specific deadline: the band was heading for a short tour of Europe in less than a month, and I'd have to be out of there by then.

That night I moved — lock, stock, and dirty Levi's — into The Basement. I parked around the corner on a side street, oozed furtively up to the house, and crept through the gate, which was open. The door to the Purple Empire stood open as well. I slunk in. Frank — for whom this was the circadian equivalent of about 9 a.m. — had his elbows propped up on his work table, coffee cup and a sausage, cheese, and pineapple pizza within easy reach, going over a new score. He glanced up. "Shut the door," he said. "Have some pizza." Then he went back to work as if I wasn't there.

In the Purple Empire the time passed as if it didn't exist, and truly, it didn't. Frank slept by day and worked by night, and since the windows were covered with heavy shutters, I never was sure what time it was out in the 'real' world. Sometimes musicians came and rehearsed, and once a very sweet young German fellow arrived to interview Frank for some existential Euro-journal, but mostly it was just Frank, the dog, and me. I had everything in there I needed to live and be happy: Frank, his music, even a bathroom — what reason was there to leave that *helioutropia* and go out where people shot and stabbed each other, where Dick Nixon was about to become President, where you were constantly being menaced by Helen Reddy's giant pulsing uvula...

I noticed that the basement hadn't changed much, if at all, since my audition there a year earlier. It was still so dim that I stumbled whenever I came in from the daylight. There was all the same gear, in essentially the same locations — the Scully four-track tape deck, a mixing board, mikes, amps, an arsenal of guitars, endless shelves full of tapes, Frank's intimidating record collection (which ran to about 10,000 items and was duly filed, headed, sub-headed, cross-referenced, and alphabetized), the *Coffee Works* right next to Frank's work area, and the Bosendorfer eight-foot concert grand. I never got to play it, since when Frank was down there he was working and I couldn't disturb him, and when he was upstairs I always felt a bit diffident about sitting down and launching into, say, George Antheil, or Frank Zappa, although I will admit I contemplated it. (Frank had once described a *very modern composition* he'd read about someplace: the performance requirements were one grand piano, one not so grand pianist, and a **chainsaw** with which the ivories were to be tickled. *"Not on my piano, you don't!"*)

Once or twice when I was alone in the basement, I crept over to the vast ebony shape, beside myself with lust, and mashed the soft pedal all the way to the floor while squeezing out a couple of apologetic little *ppp* arpeggios, just enough to ascertain that nobody had ever played it long and hard enough to break in the action. The rest of the time, I just had to lie there underneath it, panting and drooling as I suffered delirious fantasies about Frank and I playing the infamous four-handed version of *Petrouchka* with our clothes off. Hell, I'd even let him take the *primo* part. Unfortunately, my little scenario was impossible in more ways than one: Frank's involvement with keyboard instruments was limited to hunt-and-peck note-picking when he was composing and needed to figure out a melody line that wouldn't fit on the guitar. I couldn't help wondering what he was doing with a $70,000 artist instrument when a $75 spinet would have been just as good, and was reminded of the story about my favorite cellist, Jacqueline Du Pré — in one of her early concerto appearances, some crusty old conductor had listened to her tone and then took her to task: "You have such a beautiful instrument between your legs, my dear, but all you do is scratch, scratch, scratch."

The basement was anything but a monk's austere cell; the walls were festooned with artifacts, including the Fender Stratocaster Jimi Hendrix had burned at the Miami Pop Festival, original storyboards by Cal Schenkel for forthcoming film opuses, sociologically noteworthy correspondence from all over the world, photos and clippings from all phases of Frank's musical history, a rust-pocked hood from what appeared to be a once-green, '39 Chevy, hanging on the wall like a sculpture — and assorted objects which I presumed had *religious significance* to Frank, like a whole plethora of motel room keys: dozens of them, *scores* of them. Looking at them all lined up and glinting diabolically in the purple twilight, I felt my knee start jerking so intensely, I almost keeled over.

The family dog evidently suffered from both gastric and parasitic afflictions; when it wasn't farting, it was scratching fleas and farting. It seemed to like me, probably because it mistook me for a small, occasionally mobile extension of the sofa that was our mutual bed. One afternoon on the sofa I was having a vivid nightmare in which The Fiend With No Face was suffocating me with a horrible cloud of poison gas. In my dream I was somehow dying in my sleep, until I regained enough consciousness to recognize, just over my head, the posterior quarters of said canine, which was snoring away, using me as *its* sofa. At that moment I heartily envied Frank his hardcore-smoker's lack of smell.

I initially had a problem with Frank's proclivity for working when I would have ordinarily been asleep. I didn't want to complain, so the first couple of nights I tried curling up on the sofa in my sleeping bag with wads of kleenex in my ears, but my sleep was fractured by disturbing dreams, especially when he was playing the same piece of tape over and over. (*"Who's been making those new brown clouds, who's been making those clouds today?"*Try listening to *that* for five or six hours while you're trying to drift off.) Starting about the third night, I found other occupations (working through his copy of Piston's *Harmony*, relieved now and then with a dip into the racier parts of Boccaccio's *Decameron*) when Frank was toiling, and finally fell asleep in the morning, when he went back upstairs and peace reigned once again in the Purple Empire.

There always seemed to be food and drink down there. Frank was hospitably generous about sharing whatever he himself happened to be eating. Some of the things he consumed admittedly belonged more in Pathology Quarterly than "The Silver Palate Cookbook" — like the night he graciously extended half of a *signature sandwich* constructed of white bread spread with mayo and peanut butter, this covered with squashed fried bananas, and (I'm afraid I remember this all too clearly) topped off with *sardines*. I politely told him I preferred to take my chances with the pepperoni pizza that had been sitting around down there for the past couple of weeks, gradually acquiring *patina* and *complexity*.

If I had a care in the world during this time (beyond wondering whether I could manage to get by for the rest of my life on the $176 remaining from the insurance check), it wasn't that there were rapists, Republicans, and songs like the Joy of Cooking's version of "Goin' to Brownsville" in the World Outside — it was that one of these days somebody from the World Upstairs was going to come downstairs, find me huddled under the piano, and throw me out on my ear. The purple sanctum seemed to be off limits to everybody but Frank; there was a door at the top of the stairs which connected the basement to the rest of the house, but I never saw it opened from the upstairs side by anyone but Frank in the nearly four weeks I was there. I wondered if I should say something to my host about my concerns — "gee, Frank, did you ask your folks if I could stay here?" — but a plangent little inner voice warned me that some muddy depths are distinctly better left unplumbed.

Then, after I'd finally begun to be lulled into a sense of security by the comfortable if eccentric routine in the basement, one afternoon the murky currents upstairs were apparently disturbed, and the mud shark was roused at last. I was playing my L5 acoustically, my preferred method, writing a song called "Jupiter's Basement" in honor of my stay in this metaphysical Holiday Inn, when my ears caught something I'd never heard before — the muffled sound of an argument upstairs. It was only about 1:30 p.m., a little too early in the 'morning' for Frank to be up, but I could distinctly make out the sound of his voice, and he wasn't singing, neither. I'd been with him in a variety of circumstances during the past year, and I'd never once known him to raise his voice — he didn't need to, not with those death-ray eyes and his *psi*-ballistic ability to zero in for the kill on people's deepest, darkest secrets. Now he was practically shouting; this must be extremely serious business. Only his half of the contretemps was audible; he'd bellow for a number of bars, then there'd be a rest, like Music Minus One, after which he'd resume again, louder. After about ten minutes of cowering, I put down the guitar and quietly went over to where I'd stashed my belongings as neatly as possible behind the sofa. I kept most of my stuff in the trunk of my car anyway, so there wasn't much to collect, just a damp towel and toothbrush from the bathroom, and various underwear and things.

I had everything bundled up and waiting a few minutes later, when the upstairs door slammed hard and Frank came bumping down the stairs. I shuddered, wondering if somebody might not come bumping down after him with a .357 Magnum in their hand, but he was alone, and no one followed him. He was wearing just his jeans, no shirt, no shoes, and his face was an absolute thunderstorm, with green lightning bolts shooting out of his smoldering, almost black, eyes. No wonder nobody dared to challenge him: he didn't appear human, but a force of nature. His anger was so violent that he couldn't speak, although it was plain he was on fire with resentment because his old hobgoblin had attacked: his liberty had been challenged.

He sat down heavily in his work chair, unconsciously favoring his bad leg, and glared. I had worked up to telling him that I was going to leave, but when I got a close look at his face, my resolve evaporated. His resentment didn't seem to be directed at me, nor, curiously, toward his wife, but at the situation in general. Before I could say anything, he told me bluntly that I could stay on if I wanted to, that it was all right for me to be there regardless of what I might think.

In a state of emotional turmoil, I sat down next to him. On his work table was the layout for a forthcoming album cover (*The Grand Wazoo*). He'd been typing out the liner notes on his IBM Selectwriter, using only his right index finger (I don't know how he managed to do it, but he never made typos). I cleared my throat. "Frank, I don't feel good about what just happened. I appreciate your letting me stay here, but I think I should leave."

The next minute he took me completely by surprise, seizing my arm and pulling me down with him onto the floor. "Take 'em off," he said, putting his hand on the top button of my jeans. I was overwhelmed with confusion at his uncharacteristic abruptness, and for a moment I wondered if this was going to turn out to be an ugly scene, but I also sensed that he wanted validation from me and that this was his way of getting it. He never had trusted words or other people's emotional constructs, only actions, and in this instance his burning fury seemed to be so basic that it demand physical resolution. In essence, his message was something like, *Look, I just stuck my neck out defending you; show me I did the right thing.*

Eventually, feeling emotionally drained and more than a little guilty that I'd had sex under those circumstances and *enjoyed* it, I fell asleep on the sofa. The last thing I remember before I drifted off was Frank leaning over me and gently pulling my blanket up over my cold bare feet. He squeezed my toes a little as he did it, a very sweet and affectionate little gesture. Then he went back to work.

He's *sure full of surprises* , I mused, and fell into a deep, dreamless sleep. Once, when I'd asked him what he dreamed when he was asleep, he'd answered simply, "I live in my dream." When I woke up around dawn, he was still hunched over his orchestra pad.

I stayed another two weeks without further outbursts. Although

I tried to be as inconspicuous as possible when I was around and he was working, sometimes Frank would light up a smoke, put his feet on the drafting table (his bad leg, which because it had been broken was shorter than the other, was constantly throbbing, and the long hours he spent hunched over his work table gave him lower back pain too), and take a break from his labors. On one occasion he delivered an interesting little oration about Time. His theory was that human beings tried to force time to be linear and consecutive, whereas it was probably closer to a constant — in other words, there was no "now" or "then", but rather an "always." He said that everything was happening continuously, but that people were unable to grasp that concept, and so had created constructs like calendars that squeezed time into arbitrary little boxes.

When he went back to work, I sat there, half listening to him noodling on a melody line on the guitar, but mostly thinking about our relationship. The whole thing had been so peculiar and unexpected; if somebody had told me back in 1967, for example, that in 1972 I was going to be sitting there in Frank Zappa's basement under those particular circumstances, I wouldn't have believed it possible. It was about as random an occurrence as was likely to happen, or more likely not happen. Yet, Frank loved accidents and incongruities, and — if it wasn't paradoxical — sought them out constantly. In that case, maybe it was no accident that I was there.

Suddenly I sat bolt upright on the sofa and let out a whoop. It all made sense! This had all happened before...or was happening again...or should have been happening already...or something.

"What's up?" asked Frank curiously, looking up from his chart, probably wondering whether to call the paramedics.

"This whole thing — my being here — was supposed to happen," I blurted out. "I mean — it's happened before — you know what I mean?"

Frank grinned. "In which case you'd have remembered to pick up a pack of cigarettes when you go to the store," he observed. We both shared a good laugh over that one, but that didn't make it any less true.

One night Frank put on a record of Stravinsky. It was *Les Noces*, which I had never heard before. ("Now here's an entirely different sort of doo-wop," he observed, referring to the maniacal vocal parts.) I began asking him questions about Stravinsky and was impressed by his comments on the man and his work. I mentioned *L'Histoire du Soldat*, my favorite Stravinsky piece, and it turned out to be his favorite too; in fact he had recently performed the narration for a performance by Lukas Foss at the Hollywood Bowl. Out came the well-worn disc from Frank's collection, and we went over it bar by bar. I had heard the music hundreds of times before,

but
never from this per-
spective. Frank told me stories
about Stravinsky — how he'd played pickup softball games with his pals
the Marx Brothers when he lived in Beverly Hills, how he'd sometimes sit
at the lunch counter in the Thrifty drugstore on Sunset Boulevard, order
a hot fudge sundae, and when no one was looking spike it with vodka.

Frank's theories about the music, technically and historically, would
have been perspicacious and entertaining enough if he were a conven-
tionally-trained musicologist, but he had figured all this stuff out solely
by listening to the music, reading the score, and perusing a few library
books. He mentioned that his father had once offered to send him to the
Peabody Conservatory in Baltimore, but that he'd refused on the grounds
that it "would probably have perverted me." Either that, I mused, or as a
composer he might have wound up making Bartok or Varèse seem trivial
by comparison.

Without making too big a deal out of it, Frank started to play other
records from time to time, works by Webern, Varèse, Bartok, and other 20th-
century composers he had an affinity with. He would sit beside the stereo
in his work chair, sipping coffee and stopping ever so often to comment
on something of interest in the music, waving his smoking cigarette like a
pointer. He had a curious way of listening to music; he'd sit there with
one leg crossed over the other, tapping out the primary rhythm with the
motion of his right foot, the accents with his other foot, and counter
rhythms with both hands on his knees — all silently. I'd never seen anyone listen to music with such physical and mental concentration. It looked
like so much fun that I tried it myself during *L'Histoire*, and I immediately found that it almost hypnotically locked me into the music, from the basic
pulse outward. Try it yourself some time, preferably with something that
has strong counter-rhythmic interplay, and you'll see what I mean. No wonder Frank had no use for drugs!

Home, Home and Deranged

I assumed Frank was listening to music for his own entertainment, as a break from his labors, but actually he was playing it for my benefit — I think he felt it was his Christian (or pagan) duty to rescue my soul from *honky-tonk hell* . He loathed country music — that is, *white* country music; for him, country blues, a *black* form, was another story entirely — and I think he was under the impression that I didn't know about any other sort of music. He was not correct; in fact, I'd been listening to what for lack of a better term is known as 'classical' (i.e., chiefly the life work of dead males of European extraction) music since I was three or four. I'd even had a stab at performing some of it as a vocalist or percussionist. (I was too modest, or more likely ashamed, to admit these things to Frank.)

Frank was primarily interested in modern composers. He claimed he found Bach's structural approach interesting, but added that he could-n't really listen to much of the music. This made me decide his musical nature tended to be architectural rather than emotional; but just when I thought I had him pegged, he confessed, a little shamefacedly, that he loved some of Wagner's works. Hmm, I thought, that's still architectural, but you can't deny it has plenty of emotion in it, even if it's sort of on an adolescent level. Whereupon Dr. Zappa threw me yet another curve, and whipped out an album of Ravel's piano music that was so worn down the needle would barely track it. *Impressionism? Good grief!* Wisely, I ceased from further conclusion-jumping about Frank's underlying musical aesthetic. "If it sounds good to you, then it's good music," shrugged the perverse Professor. Like some of his other observations, this seemed absurd on the surface, but turned out to be a tough theorem to refute.

But the most moving moment in the Mad Maestro's Music Appreciation course came when he played me Bartok's Third Piano Concerto. "The first time I heard the main melody in the first movement of this thing, I almost (*now don't laugh*) cried," he said with a fierce shyness when he put on the record, just daring me to snicker. It was the far-thest thing from my mind; when the theme in question came blasting out through the studio monitors, my throat and chest became so tight with tears — not of grief, but of awe — that I couldn't breathe. It seemed to me as if Bartok, in the first few minutes of that first movement, had personified humankind's highest and most exalted potentialities, thrown into noble relief against the shadow of modern horror and disillusionment. There aren't any words for that sort of thing; only music can describe it, and for me, the Third Piano Concerto still describes it more eloquently than any-thing else I've heard.

Looking at Frank, I saw that the main theme — a rapid, fluent cascade of notes in the Hungarian mode, first stated simply, then developed into awesome multi-dimensonality — had entirely taken him over. There was none of the usual droll commentary this time. In a trance, his hand tapping out the rhythms on his knee, he leaned forward into the music, so intent on its every nuance that in the ashtray beside him his untouched cigarette slowly burned down to the filter. As the work progressed, he gradually disappeared into it, finally becoming one with Bartok's magnanimous universe, leaving behind the suffocating meanness and mediocrity both composers had struggled so much of their lives to escape.

I hope Frank is floating around somewhere like that now, only with some *expanded opportunities for glandular recreation* mixed in with the hifalutin stuff.

Then one night, with studied casualness, he asked me if I'd ever composed any "serious" music. I guess we'd progressed to the point where he figured I was ready to quit *"pooting around"* and get to work. I didn't know what to say; I didn't consider myself any sort of "serious" composer. Feeling quite embarrassed, I finally came clean about my experiences at El Camino, and confessed that I'd given up studying composition because it required a stability I seemed to, er, lack at the moment.

I had a tape of a piano composition, "Opus One," which had earned me an A in my Composition class at El Camino. The assignment had been to build an original etude from a pre-existing theme, and the theme I had chosen was the opening notes of the piano solo on Frank's composition "Little House I Used to Live In". By definition, "Opus One" was a very derivative piece, and I was no longer sure what I thought of it, but I played it for Frank so that he could at least see I'd been involved in semi-serious musical study. To my surprise, he seemed to like it a lot. I guess it made him realize I wasn't really an ignorant *shitkicker/hillbilly-type person* after all, even if I did insist on wearing those *poot-stompers*. I suspect it also elicited another realization: the fact that his music was a real inspiration for me. That was something I'd never been able to put into words, but he could hear it for himself on the tape of "Opus One", and as much as he tried to hide behind that wry, ironic, Professor Pootmeister facade, I think he was actually *touched* .

After hearing the tape, he mentioned that if I felt like *whipping up a little something* , I could bring it along to the next Grand Wazoo rehearsal and hear what it sounded like. It took me about 24 hours before the bomb dropped, but when I realized what his offer represented, I turned into a tornado. I grabbed my L5 (which I didn't plug into an amp because I was concerned about making too much noise) and Frank's big orchestra scratch pad, along with his Range and Transposition Guide, and began scribbling away during the daytime when he was asleep upstairs. I worked feverishly all day, every day, putting the guitar back in its place and hiding my day's work when Frank came down at night. Finally, a week later, on the night before the next day's Grand Wazoo rehearsal, I told him I'd jotted down a little piece, and if he'd been serious about his offer...

"What you got?" he asked.

Trying not to let my hands shake, I handed him the pages from the orchestra pad. It was a very little piece, maybe a minute and a half long, scored for oboe, bass clarinet, bassoon, trombone, marimba, guitar, bass guitar, and drums. I'd called it "Statement of Earnings."

Frank looked at the title and grinned, the humor not lost on him. "'Statement of Earnings' — *hmm*." He ran his eye down the score, analyzing it. Without further comment, he said, "You better copy the parts," and gestured toward a stack of blank charts and a copying pen. I stayed up until seven the next morning, writing out each separate part and transposing the horn charts. Because I hadn't been able to use the piano to compose on, the harmonic structure was almost medieval, based on the way a suspended chord sounded on the guitar. In my inexperience, I had written passages that made for impossible fingerings on some of the horns, and in my haste I'd copied in a bunch of wrong notes. It represented the very bottom, dumbest level of sub-student work, and Frank obviously recognized that the minute he looked at it, but he also knew that the only way I'd learn anything was if I was directly confronted by my own mistakes.

In the afternoon I waited until Frank had been gone half an hour, then headed down to the Temple of the Grand Wazoo with my precious bundle of charts on the seat beside me. I almost didn't make it to the rehearsal: I was woolgathering so bad that I ran a red light as I was making a left turn at the intersection of Sunset and Crescent Heights, only narrowly avoiding intimate involvement with an RTD bus and a couple of BMWs. As I went puttering off down Sunset, I vaguely wondered what all the squealing brakes were about back there.

I took a seat in the front of the rehearsal hall and waited while Frank ran the band through several numbers. Usually every aspect of the rehearsals was fascinating to me, but not today, for some reason. It seemed like a fucking *eternity* . Finally, though, Frank motioned me up to the conducting stand. "Pass out the parts," he said.

I went out and handed the players the charts. Then I came back and spread my master score across the stand. Immediately, the musicians began to shout questions and complaints at me. "This note is out of my range,"

"This run is all little finger," ""Is this an E-flat or an E natural here?" Frank shot me a wry look. *"Does this kind of life look interesting to you?"* he mugged. I answered as many of the questions as I could, and then Frank mercifully stepped in and explained to them that this was my maiden effort in the orchestral realm, so they wouldn't keep bugging me.

Then there was another little problem: I'd written the guitar part for Frank; in fact, the whole piece was based around his most characteristic harmonic element, both as a guitarist and a composer — the suspended chord, a chord with no major or minor third, just modal tones. I started to hand him the chart, but he shook his head and told me to give it to Tony Duran, the Wazoo's rhythm guitarist. I tried to explain that the piece had been conceived as a little concerto for him and chamber orchestra, but he still wouldn't play it. Probably because there was a guitar solo in the piece, he didn't want to have it thrown at him in front of all the hotshots he had working for him. What if he made a complete ass of himself playing something that stupidly simple? (He knew his limitations as a musician, and mine as a composer, I had to admit.) I'd just have to be satisfied with employing him as *celebrity page-turner* while I conducted.

"Here you go," he said, handing me his baton. "Count it off." And he looked down at my score — *my* score — and waited.

I counted off four bars for nothing, then raised the baton. My God — there it was — *my opening chord*. I felt as if I'd just created the heavens and the earth. No drug could produce an intoxication as powerful as this. There were a million things going on at once, and I couldn't keep track of them all — I didn't dare, or there would have been a mass derailment. Right off I noticed that the voicings stuck out and sounded much more eccentric played on the different horns than they had as notes on the guitar. Dimly I began to understand that writing for timbre and texture was a whole art I didn't have a clue about. Whoops, here we were at the bottom of the first page. Frank flipped it and we went on. The marimba player fluffed the ostinato in bar 38; the oboe hit a series of truly ugly D-sharps (my copying mistake coming home to roost — *ouch!*); here came the guitar solo. Top of page three, bar 76, drum solo, damn, should've made that eight bars instead of four. Christ! why hadn't I realized that that syncopation was an eighth note, not a sixteenth? Oh boy...it's the grand finale, every instrument for himself, let 'er rip! Wow! That's the wildest-sounding thing I've ever heard in my life! And finally the coda, the head again, sounds like the goddamn gates of Heaven are opening and the saints are rolling in! *Yes.* ..oh Lord, God, yes!!!

I cut off the last bar with a flourish and lowered the baton. There was a little applause from a few of the people who hadn't been playing. Nice folks, I thought, knowing I hadn't deserved it. I handed the baton back to Frank, who nodded at me gravely and made a little bow, and stumbled to the back of the hall, completely swamped by sensations. It had only taken a minute and a half, but that 90 seconds had unrolled like a scroll into eternity. Now I knew what I was going to do with the rest of my life. *I was going to spend it waving a white stick at a bunch of men and women in evening clothes in an empty concert hall while they turned my little dots-on-paper into masses of very dense air.*

People were talking to me, asking me questions, but I didn't comprehend and couldn't answer. I mumbled something, went out and got into my car, and drove around for hours, the music still ringing in my ears like the roar of the ocean.

It was approaching the time when the band was going to leave for Europe. The tour wasn't a long one, just four or five dates, and I got the feeling Frank would have been willing to take me along as music librarian, if I'd asked him. But when I checked with the bureaucrats downtown, I learned that a passport application took nearly a month to process. There wasn't enough time for that. I cursed their red tape, but there it was.

On my last night in the basement, I sat around talking to Frank. He was able to foretell the fate of the Grand Wazoo in advance; it was going to break up immediately after the tour. In my case, the future was a considerably lesser-known quantity. Frank was in his paternalistic mood (darn!), sitting back in his chair with his feet up on the control board and frowning at me like some poor plumber forced to face the fact that he has stumbled upon the Eternally Leaking Faucet. Sometimes, when he didn't think I was looking, I'd caught him regarding me with a mixture of exasperation and pity. He was probably shaking his head over the fact that I reminded him of himself when he was 18 — only I most likely didn't have his illustrious future in front of me.

"So what are your plans after this?" he asked. It wasn't so much a question as a statement.

All of a sudden I was seized by a bright and desperate idea. I knew that when he got back from the Grand Wazoo Farewell Tour, he was going to have some down time. I also had the feeling that he was about as approachable this minute as he was ever likely to be, for whatever reason.

"Frank," I said, swallowing fast, before rationality could take over and spoil my plan, "I think you should produce my album."

He looked as if he wished he could yank on the tap with a spanner and stop the drip for once and for all. "I'm not going to have the time," he began, but I was ready for that.

"Look," I said, "I'll have the songs all ready to go by the time you get back from Europe. We don't need to hire the guys from the Grand Wazoo. You and I can play just about everything; all we'd need is a drummer at most. We can record everything in a couple of weeks, on the cheap."

Frank smelled a rat, and not a hot one, either. "Why should I want to block out the time to do this?" he asked warily.

"Because it's time I made my first record, and I want you to produce it," I said baldly.

Most people dislike being cornered; Frank absolutely hated it, because it rarely happened to him, and on the rare occasions when it did, none of his usual tactics worked. He growled, "What makes you think I don't have other things to do when I get back?", but I saw the chink in the brick wall and pressed on into the home stretch. "Look, at least let me demo up the songs. You can listen to them when you get back, and see what you think."

Of course I had no idea how I was going to accomplish this. In order to make the demos, I first had to compose the songs in question. Oh well — one thing at a time.

Frank was starting to get very tired. "We'll see," he ventured, and I jumped up and threw my arms around him. "Oh boy! Great!" I yelled. He shook his head and started to put up a warning hand, but I stopped him. "I ought to let you get back to what you're doing," I said selflessly, looking heavenward. "I know you've got to get packed and everything, and, uh, I guess I ought to be doing the same." I really was sad to be leaving the basement; Frank must have seen that emotion on my face, because he put his arm around me and let me sit down in his lap. After that, neither of us thought about the album project again for quite a while.

CHAPTER 10

Statement of Earnings

I'd been too busy working on "Statement of Earnings" to look for a job or a place to stay, but fortunately Ruth and Ian Underwood (probably with a little nudging from Frank) graciously agreed to let me crash at their place with the usual half-hearted caveat that it was "just until I could find something permanent". *Right...*

The scene at their house in North Hollywood (it was across the street from the house where Nathanael West had been living when he and his wife were killed in a car accident in Mexico — on December 21, 1940, Frank's birthday) was pleasant and, under the circumstances, fairly normal. Ian spent his days fooling with synthesizers; he was getting a leg up in the film and TV scoring world. Ruth was a classically-trained percussionist who had made an appearance on the early Mothers album "Uncle Meat" as well as in *200 Motels*. At that point, she was in *career limbo*, although a year or so later she would be back working with Frank, and would go on to become one of his most well-known sidepersons.

Ruth and I sometimes sipped Constant Comment (or at least she did; I had my own private stash of Medaglia d'Oro) and talked "girl talk," a new pastime for me. However, our chats encompassed a rather different universe than the term might suggest — we were more likely to be discussing Harry Breuer or the logistics of constructing a percussion system that operated two timpani, three gongs, and a row of temple blocks with one beater, as we were to be gossiping about how lousy X. looked in a bikini or who was messing around with whom. (We *did* gossip, of course, but it was a guilty pleasure for both of us; we had to fight off the nagging feeling that we should somehow have been *bigger than that*.) We were both highly verbal, and for some reason we tended to sound like six or eight people rather than two when we had these little chats; multiple personalities, maybe. We agreed that Frank was mighty lucky he'd never had to cope with having both of us in the band at the same time; it would have driven him completely *around the bend*.

Ruth and I also had something else in common, unfortunately for her — we loved Frank's music and we both knew it firsthand. At that point, though, both she and Ian were going through a phase of trying to break free of the *noxious Zappa influence* and get on with their lives. I was probably the worst roommate the two of them could have had right then. I was forbidden to utter *That Name* in the house; if I *had* to say it, I was obliged to go out in the backyard, away from the windows, and mumble it under my breath. Eventually I would be able to understand extremely well what they were going through, but that wouldn't be for a couple more years; as it was, I sadistically enjoyed teasing them by referring to Frank in Lovecraftian terms as *"He Who Shall Remain Nameless"* and by talking about him in elaborately periphrastic third person. Maybe I wasn't being a considerate guest, but I couldn't help it (not that that excused my conduct).

Ruth and Ian, like many others in that bygone era, were vegetarians. They were also very hospitable hosts, and always set a place for me at the table. My idea of a balanced meal, meanwhile, was (and still is) a couple of double chili cheeseburgers. (Frank had once drawn a little caricature of me with a burger in each hand: *a balanced meal*.) One day at breakfast (I didn't mind breakfast; after all, cereal is cereal, whether it's Sugar Pops and Golden Creme slightly outdated half and half, or certified Vermont-grown triple organic granola 'n' genuine positively *non-dairy soy fiber whitener*), Ruth announced that for dinner that very night I was going to have the chance of a lifetime to attain *nutritive and culinary nirvana* (and here I'd always thought those two things were mutually exclusive). She would be spending all day toiling in the kitchen to produce (timpani roll, please) SOYBEAN STEW, and the pleasure of my company was definitely requested at dinner this evening.

I quietly went out and grabbed a burger and fries for lunch so I

110

could maintain my decorum at the dinner table. But when the grand moment came, I realized I was still going to have to perform. All eyes were on me as the steaming bowl of lumpy brown semisolids was ceremoniously placed before me. Ruth handed me a spoon. I took a deep breath, closed my eyes, and plunged the spoon into the muck. It resisted slightly, making a muffled sucking sound. I scraped some of the more solid part onto the tip of the spoon, raised it, forced it between my lips, and swallowed it. (*You've had worse things in your mouth, for Chrissakes* , I remonstrated internally.)

"Well, what do you think?" Ruth demanded.

"OK, OK!" I spluttered, spraying khaki goo halfway across the table. "I promise I'll never mention *(urp!)* That Name again as long as I'm here — honest to God!"

Soybean stew never again reared its organic head while I was there. That Name was equally conspicuous in its absence from my conversation, even parenthetically.

Meanwhile, I was taking my demo seriously, whatever opinion Frank might have had of the whole business. I sat down at Ian's Mason

©1995 NIGEY LENNON

Ian and Ruth Underwood

and Hamlin grand and went into mass production. Within a week I had eight songs finished, in the form of chord charts and lyrics. Then I tortuously recorded them on a purloined Akai stereo quarter-track tape recorder at 7 1/2 i.p.s., laying down one instrumental or vocal part at a time and subsequently 'ping-ponging' the aggregation of tracks back onto one channel, until I had all the parts accounted for. It didn't really sound *too* bad, considering the primitive technology I was forced to utilize.

There were three vocal numbers, and five instrumentals. I performed all the vocals and played most of the instruments, with a couple of exceptions: an improvised synthesizer/*musique concrete* (screwdriver and metal stool) section by Don Preston on an instrumental called "Moto Guzzi", and a space-jazz Fender Rhodes piano accompaniment by my old high school sidekick Dave Benoit on a vocal selection called "Heavy Lip Action" (the concept of the song had come to me while witnessing the *multiplicity of labial torments* stoically endured by Earle Dumler, the Wazoo's oboe, English horn, and sarrusophone player).

At this point in his career still a struggling lounge lizard, Dave was trying to compose music for 'real' instruments, and when he heard about my religious experience with "Statement of Earnings," he'd started showing up at Wazoo rehearsals, interrogating the musicians and generally making his presence known. After a couple of these appearances, Frank took me aside and asked me who he was, whereupon Dave waltzed over, stuck out his hand, and intoned, "Pleased to meet you, Mr. Zappa — I'm David Benoit, the composer." Frank looked over at me; I rolled my eyes, as if to say *This wasn't* my *idea, honest.* "Well, let's hear it, then," said Frank resignedly. "Pass out the parts." It turned out to be a "Suite for Electric Piano and Acoustic Orchestra" in three — count 'em, three — movements. Guess who the Horrorwitz in question was? He made *me* conduct while he walloped the (plastic) ivories; he'd just happened to bring along his own Fender Rhodes piano. Frank woke up about halfway through the middle *Larghetto non troppo mortuis in extremis* , looked at the clock, and coughed. "Thank you veddy much, Mr. Composer," he said, warningly. Yes, Dave definitely owed me a favor.

As far as the actual album was concerned, I intended some of the songs to have guest vocalists; one of the vocals, called "Ruin," was a mutant blues number designed to be apocalyptically howled by Captain Beefheart, if we could somehow lure him down from the hippie hamlet of Ben Lomond in the Santa Cruz Mountains, where he was living in colorful poverty; and another was a duet for myself and Frank, sort of a surreal doo-wop tune with pseudo-Stravinsky vocal harmonies. Of course, I had no intention of playing any of the guitar solos on this little biscuit. That would have been schlepping anthracite to Newcastle, under the circumstances. On one of the instrumentals, I'd planned to sucker Frank into actually playing Western swing without him being aware of it; I'd taken the structure of "Steel Guitar Rag" (which itself was based on standard blues changes anyway) and perverted the voicings until Leon McAuliffe's mother wouldn't have recognized them, thrown in some 'tuplet sforzandos on the offbeats (always lots of fun when you're in cut time), and voila! *Mutant guitar strangler's delight!* (The title of the opus was "Chicken Fried Sex".) Frank wouldn't know what hit him. Hell, if he could take '50s doo-wop and subject it to Dr. Zurkon's Secret Formula on "Ruben and the Jets," I could do the same thing with '40s hayseed-hipster music on *my* record.

As soon as Frank was back from Europe and had had a few days to decompress, I called him and let him know the demo was ready. He sounded somewhat grouchy, but he told me to bring it over. Within a half hour of our phone conversation, I was sitting in the basement with him. He put on my tape and gave it his usual intent listen. Then he turned to me, folded his arms, and declaimed:

"This stuff is so *off the wall* nobody's going to get it in a million years. You'd be lucky if you sold ten copies of the thing."

I bowed my head humbly and thanked him, adding that, coming from him, I took it as a compliment.

Next we started quibbling and wrangling with logistics and, worse, numbers. I wanted to get right to work on the album; in fact I immediately put in a call to Cal Schenkel, the artist who had done most of Frank's album art, and asked him to start working on a design for my album cover. But Frank took the wind right out of my sails. "You've got things ass backward," he grumbled. "I haven't even figured out if I'm going to be able to produce it yet, and you're thinking about the cover." He then asked if I had any idea of what the budget for this vinyl extravaganza was likely to be. I told him I didn't — wasn't that his department?

Poor Frank. Sighing and adjusting the visor of his imaginary green eyeshade, he proceeded to explain the facts of life to me: Albums cost money to produce — more than I probably realized. Even an El Cheapo production would run between fifteen and twenty thousand by the time you figured in the engineer's salary, the cost of raw tape (at 30 i.p.s., it took a lot of tape to

113

make a 40-or-so-minute album, what with all the, er, false starts and uh, worthless takes there were likely to be in, um, this case), incidental musicians, recording and mixdown time, payments to Schenkel for artwork, mastering and refs, pressing costs, etc., etc.. Now if my hypothetical album (I noticed he stressed the modifier 'hypothetical' very pointedly) were to sell, say, 5,000 copies ("I'm feeling very *expansive* tonight, ahem") at the profitability level of 75 cents apiece, it didn't take Dr. Einstein to comprehend the *algebra ad absurdum* here:

"You're going to wind up owing the record company money," he concluded.

"But *you're* the record company," I said.

Frank gave me a long-suffering look. "Glad you picked up on that," he said wearily.

Frank actually had some other things to do besides work on my big hit album. He had assembled a new band, and was starting to rehearse with it. Both Ruth and Ian were in it — so much for the *"He Who Shall Remain Nameless"* stuff. It even had Jean-Luc Ponty playing violin, and George Duke on keyboards. I didn't want to get sucked into the old black hole of living at rehearsals again, but gravity was my enemy. Ruth, who was an ex-New Yorker, didn't drive. Since I had a car of sorts, and — let's be honest about this, folks — time on my hands, I somehow got elected transportation captain. The new rehearsal facility was on Sunset Boulevard near Bronson Avenue in Hollywood, and on the way over the hill from the Valley, we'd stop off in Laurel Canyon and pick up Jeff Simmons. He had moved back to L.A. from Seattle and was playing bass in the group. We'd go chugging down Laurel Canyon Boulevard in my battered black '62 Fairlane (which was mostly held together with little orange decals that said "Wazoo," and of course my "Captain Beefheart for President" bumper sticker). Ruth's road case full of cymbals, gongs, hand percussion, and miscellaneous paraphernalia, crammed in beside her in the back seat and totally blocking my view out of the rear window, was so heavy it made the wobbly suspension sag even further; while up front Simmons, in shades, five o'clock shadow, and knitted cap, would be riding shotgun with his coffin case between his knees, occasionally rousing himself from his personal twilight to hurl highly random epithets out the window: "Hey, Itchy Dean!", "Feature your hurt, or *punt*!". Other motorists gave us a very wide berth, for some reason.

The rehearsal space was a lot like a blimp hangar. It had probably started life as a sound stage 20 or 30 years earlier, but at some point in recent history it had been rehabilitated, and now it provided a reasonable facsimile of the performing conditions in a large nightclub or a small hall, minus only the kid on reds puking on your shoes from the first row. (The drinks were supplied by the liquor store a few doors down.) There was a long stage with a full complement of lighting and sound reinforcement gear, two-story-high, sliding load-in doors, and the best central air conditioning in town. In front was a warren of offices, the headquarters of Frank's new record company, DiscReet. (Alarmed about his evidently declining morals, I had a little talk with him: first he'd been Bizarre, then Straight, and now he was downright DiscReet. Had he no shame? "Whaddaya think I am — some kind of dinosaur?" was his growled rejoinder.)

Despite my strong misgivings, I soon had my work cut out for me. It was like the Grand Wazoo, only more so. When Frank wanted Ruth to pick up, say, a parade drum or a couple dozen pairs of Good Vibes mallets in time for the next rehearsal, off we'd go to Professional Drums on Vine Street — in my car. A steady procession of amps and anvil cases soon reduced my back seat to a puree of ravaged vinyl. Because I was a guitar player and familiar with Frank's equipment, so to speak, there were courtesy trips to Guitar Center, or to the independent technicians who worked on his instruments. Once or twice I even got dragooned into going to the Players Motel, next to Local 47 of the Musicians' Union on Vine, to pick up or deliver out-of-town musicians who were trying out for the band.

Frank was collaborating on effects devices with a fellow named Bob Easton, an electronics wizard who ran a secret lab near Rampart and Temple. Easton, with the backing of people like Frank, had been attempting to put into production a number of intriguing 'black boxes', most of which went beyond the merely quixotic into the realm of the *truly sonically demented.* At rehearsal one day, I was promised a demonstration of the Electro-Wagnerian Emancipator, which theoretically was supposed to take a single note and transform it into a chord, the harmonic structure and timbre of which could be as complex and bewildering as the operator wished. Easton carried in a nondescript, medium-sized black crate with a row of knobs on the front, Frank plugged his guitar into it, there was 45 minutes worth of studious tweaking and twiddling — then horrid noises, frowns, and hushed conference back and forth — and the experiment was finally determined to be a failure. Frank eventually socked

$40,000 into R&D on the Emancipator, but the appliance was never deemed publicly operable.

Frank had been composing and accumulating a great deal of music, and when he had rehearsed the band sufficiently, he started recording them. I decided to keep him under close surveillance so that my big album project wouldn't get shoved too far toward that dreaded 'back burner' from whence there was no return.

Frank didn't seem to have any objection to my sitting near his elbow in the control room, even if I was there as long as he was. There was bound to come a time when the last cigarette in the pack was gone, or when the mundane but vital subject of pizza, or cheeseburgers, reared its ugly head. Once in awhile he'd shoot me a look, as if to ask "Don't you have anything better to be doing?" The truth was, I couldn't think of anything more exciting than being there watching him make an album. Since I'd never seen him operate in the studio, I found the experience immensely edifying, well worth the 'tuition' of all those trips to the liquor store or the fast-food emporium. In the recording studio, he really *was* Dr. Zurkon in his lab in Happy Valley, distilling the essence of that sound, mixing it with this other sound over here, spending eight or ten hours to capture 60 seconds of audio exactly the way he wanted it. His recording m.o. was identical with his sexual philosophy — obsessiveness, situationism, attention to detail, pushing the envelope until it mutated into — anything he felt like.

In recording the album that was eventually called "Over-Nite Sensation," he used several facilities. One of them, Whitney Studios, was in Glendale. By this time I was living in Silver Lake, in a one-bedroom flat in a crumbling, turn-of-the-century house. It was a 15-minute drive from Silver Lake to Glendale, and there was a Mexican take-out stand right at the midpoint of the trip. They served the greasiest *carnitas* burritos this side of heaven. Now if they could just remember to leave out the fucking onions...

At Whitney there was a fairly decent pipe organ. The studio was owned by the Mormon church, and maybe they were hoping that someday they'd be able to rent it to the Mormon Tabernacle Choir. Instead, they got distinctly unholy clients like Frank Zappa. Frank had lots of fun with that organ. Once or twice I got on the thing and demonstrated some of its more amusing tricks to him. He wound up having George

Duke record a frenetic solo on it during the song "Fifty-Fifty". As I may have stated earlier, Frank wasn't much of a keyboard player. He looked upon two-handed pianists with a kind of incredulous awe. But no one was better equipped to appreciate the textural and symbolic properties of a big organ, no matter how many hands were on it.

Frank, at the moment, didn't have any full-time vocalists (he didn't consider himself a vocalist, just a guy who made "mouth noises," and low grade ones at that). For the album, he brought in a revolving array of hired lungs to assist him in the vocal department. I'm not sure where he found some of them. One chap was a total dipsomaniac, although Frank didn't know it until it was apparently too late. I got my first inclination that there might be a problem when I showed up at the studio around one in the afternoon and found this character sharing a bottle of Pouilly Fuisse with Jean-Luc Ponty, the French violinist; Ponty took a few urbane sips from a Dixie cup — whereupon Mr. Dip upended the bottle and chugged the remainder in one swell *floop!*

By the time Frank needed Mr. Dip to record his vocal track, there had been numerous surreptitious trips to the liquor store around the corner, and a fair amount of Courvoisier under the bridge. He vanished into the isolation booth, and you never heard such howling in your life. After the 20th and final take, he took a couple of wavering steps backward, put out an unsteady hand to stop himself, then passed out cold on the floor. Nonetheless, Frank evidently approved of Mr. Dip's vocal qualities, because he later took Mr. Dip on tour — a very serious mistake, as he discovered. Before too long, Mr. Dip's liquor tab in the various motel lounges had far exceeded his per diem and was reaching toward the National Deficit. Frank promptly gave him the sack, and not the dry sack, either. Like a lot of drunks, Mr. Dip actually had a certain psychotic charm when he was sober. He heard my demo and, by this time having been excused from Frank's employ, wanted to put together a band with me. When I mentioned it to Frank, he strongly suggested that I give it serious thought and then *just say "no" to Mr. Dip* ."He'd end up costing you in the long run," he said with a bitter little laugh, in the tone of *one who knows*.

Another studio Frank used belonged to a formerly very big husband-and-wife R&B singing team who were now reduced to playing oldies revues in Europe. This studio was right on the edge of L.A.'s African-American district, and the scene there was rather circuslike, with individuals in tribal regalia and fascinating hair wandering into the control room, pausing to listen, making picturesque comments, and then drifting back out again.

Frank was working on a song called "Dirty Love," a get-down

117

shuffle with a funky clavinet vamp and biting guitar. The lyrics, sung by Frank, represented his sexual and emotional philosophy in, shall we say, the most basic of terms. I thought that what the tune needed was a down-home kind of backup chorus — grunts, groans, the sound of sweat dripping down the walls. Almost jokingly, I told him I could work out some background vocal parts. I was a little surprised, but he let me overdub three backup vocal tracks.

When he played them back with the rest of the song, it was obvious that, although my vocal arrangement was effective, my very white-sounding voice just didn't cut it. I sounded about as black and libidinous as Roberta Flack. As we were falling all over the control room laughing about it, Mrs. Ex-Big R&B Singer came strolling in. She was short, well built, and good natured. Frank graciously offered her a chair (he was a hardcore R&B fan, and, at least to my eyes, seemed to have more than a superficial rapport with black musicians) and let her sit there and listen to the backup tracks too.

"Ssshit, man," she pronounced suddenly, "I could do that blindfolded with a broomstick up my ass." And she began to laugh wildly.

"I ain't got a broomstick, but I think there's a rancid bandana around here someplace," said Frank with a wink. He helped her out into the studio and put the headphones on her. Then he ran the tape of the song with the lead vocal foremost in the mix so she could get in sync with it.

It only took her one pass to nail all my vocal harmonies, and another to lay down her first track. The other two followed in short order, grunts, groans, and all. Her three overdubbed parts somehow managed to sound like a whole gospel chorus in the throes of sanctified estrus. (*"Pa-raise Jee-zus! Get down on yo' knees, sister, and testify!"*)

In the control room, I looked over at Frank, grinned, and shrugged. He grinned back, then regained his composure and raced to adjust the furiously slapping VU meters on the board. A few years later, Mrs. Ex-Big R&B Singer left her husband, struck out on her own, and became a household name singing Top 40 pop. A feature film was even made about her life and struggles. Whenever I heard her voice on the radio, I was reminded of how she'd recorded my backup vocals on "Dirty Love" — a sterling example of socio-musical incongruity if ever there was one.

I reminded Frank about my album project so often that he finally agreed to cut a test track. He had finished "Over-Nite Sensation" and had a European tour coming up, so we had to work fast. Right away we ran into 'creative differences'; he wanted to record a vocal, and I had my heart set on an instrumental, with him playing the guitar. I had written an elaborate instrumental called "Marimba Green," with a marimba solo for Ruth Underwood, and a *very* long guitar solo. Since I'd finished it after making my original demo, all I had were the charts for it, nothing in recorded form. I brought the music to a rehearsal one day and gave it to Frank to check out, hoping it would impress him so much that he'd want to get right to work on recording it.

The first thing he did when he got my charts was frown, pick up a pencil, and start to scribble on them. I had forgotten what a stickler for detail he was. He proofread steadily during the dead spots in the rehearsal, keeping an eagle eye especially out for rhythmic inaccuracies, and by the time rehearsal was over, there were dozens of tiny, precise, annoying cor-

© 1995 LIONEL ROLFE

Frank's choice for the back cover photo of my 'imaginary album'. It featured a number of 'secret clues' and in-jokes pertaining to our relationship -- I was wearing his socks, playing a Gibson 335 like the one that got burned at Montreux, posing in front of a Studebaker Hawk ("Billy the Mountain"), etc.

rections throughout my manuscript. Not one of them was superfluous. I still have that pencil-ridden manuscript stashed away, and every ten years or so I take it out, look at it, and wince. It keeps me humble.

We never did make the album. The more we tried to see eye to eye, the less we agreed. At some point I realized that Frank didn't want to come right out and say 'No' to me, but he really didn't want to go through with it. In retrospect, I suspect he was right. When Frank assumed the role of producer, he really took over; he didn't work *with* something, or someone, as much as he worked *on* it, or them, and he generally wasn't satisfied until he'd wrung the last ounce of *audio verite* out of the situation. For my part, I was idiosyncratic and inflexible — not a good combination. Who knows what mutant offspring our collaboration would have wrought? Maybe this ill-begotten child of Patsy Montana and Anton Webern would have crept up on one or both of us and murdered us in our sleep. I never found out; I decided to let Frank off the hook. Besides, in my fantasy my *super-bitchen debut album* was far more satisfying than it probably would have ever been on cold, hard vinyl. You especially oughta hear all those *imaginary guitar solos* !

CHAPTER 11

No Commercial Potential

I spent most of 1973 with London as my base of operations, shopping around my demo tape to various British and European record companies. A couple of labels, catching a whiff of the Zappa aroma enveloping the project, expressed an interest, and I got all excited — until my agent explained what was going on. The world economy was beginning to slump as a result of the Middle East oil embargo. At least one of the record labels in question was just minutes away from going out of business — the idea was for them to run up a big deficit by signing countless eminently unrecordable acts (*like me*) with no intent of doing anything with them, and then declare bankruptcy, citing the negative cash flow of 'unprofitable investments'. My youthful idealism, already a little pitted, was further corroded by this exposure to the Real World of Capitalism. Frank was right, as fucking always — my demo was phenomenally non-commercial. I didn't write love songs, and I didn't sing enough to be considered a *girl artist* by any self-respecting record company in the '70s. (*Carly Simon* was then the industry benchmark for female musical achievement.) *Five instrumentals??!* My guitar playing just added insult to injury. It's so depressing being 20 years ahead of your time.

About midway through my London exile, Frank and the band came through to play the Wembley Pool. I called him at the hotel to say hello. He sounded extremely grumpy and short, but he did agree (*gee thanks, Frank*) to let me ride to that night's gig on the band bus. He sulked all night in a wonderfully autistic fashion. I think he wished I was back in L.A. where he could get at me whenever he felt like it, even if all he might feel like doing was ignoring me.

Before the show I sat with Jean-Luc Ponty in the Wembley Pool canteen, drinking Bird's Instant Coffee Powder in lukewarm water and discussing classical violin repertory. Frank stomped by on his way backstage, saw us debating the respective merits of Menuhin vs. Heifetz, and snorted. There was a gal following determinedly right behind him. I don't remember if she was a redhead or not. He barely said goodnight to me when I got off the bus at the end of the night.

When I'd finally had my fill of *broadening experiences* — like the cholera epidemic in Naples (the joke was "*See Naples and die*"), the curious mental state that derived from the knowledge that as long I was in Europe I'd have to use wax paper instead of Charmin, and the sybaritic pleasures of existence in damp, uninsulated buildings *with no heating in freezing weather* — I ceased drifting about the Continent and returned to the land of cheeseburgers, central air, and long lines at the gas pumps. Once back in L.A., I found a job in Encino as a live-in companion to a well-to-do woman with Meniere's disease (the one where your inner ear messes up your sense of balance and you spend a lot of time falling over). My duties consisted of driving her to and from her office near downtown L.A. and keeping her company. In exchange, I had my own room, grub, cigarette money, and a deceptively nondescript-looking 1966 Mustang convertible with a racing engine (a relic of my boss' former marriage; her ex had been a 'weekend warrior'). I had lots of time to work on my music and writing, freed for once from the pressures of '*objectionable reality.*'

Since the album project was basically a dead issue, I wanted to keep from being sucked back into Frank's force field. I attended a couple of rehearsals, trying to remain on genial terms with him, but out of his grip. I hadn't been up to the Purple Empire since our last album project meeting, and I quit calling up and inviting myself over there. Hoping I could focus on my own work, I lay low.

Forget it. Somehow I wound up being sucked back into the whirlpool. Sometimes Ruth needed a ride, sometimes there was a guitar emergency, other times I just happened to be in the vicinity of the rehearsal hall, so I might as well stop by... I suppose I could have quit the whole scene cold turkey, but my best friend (Ruth) and whatever Frank was, were too important to me.

Frank was still limping by without an 'official' lead vocalist at this point, but he was thinking about staging a lengthy piece called "Hunchentoot," an essay in the world of cheesy sci-fi he so dearly loved, and he needed vocalists to handle the lead parts, especially the title role of Drakma, Queen of the Universe. Ruth wanted me to try out for the part. I had my doubts; I was getting to the point where I didn't want to be close to Frank. Often it seemed to me that he just wasn't the same person I'd met in 1970. The Rainbow Theater incident had left a permanent impression on his character, and now he was sarcastic and cynical a considerable part of the time.

Not long before this, Frank had met a bubbly music journalist (*three guesses what color hair she had*) during a tour of Australia. Everybody in the band was amazed when, after the tour, he'd flown her to Los Angeles, put her up at an undisclosed location, and continued to carry on with her, hot and heavy. It didn't go on for more than a couple of weeks, but since I was hanging around rehearsals, I had a front-row seat for the proceedings, and I had to admit it hurt like hell. I'd never stopped loving Frank's music, and to a certain extent, I still loved him; I didn't realize how much of a problem I still had until I saw him in the flesh, oozing all over his buxom paramour from Down Under. Although I felt a catty sort of satisfaction when Nelly Bly was unceremoniously packed off to the bush again after Frank grew bored with her massive charms, the whole experience was a painful reminder that I had no desire to go on tour with him and see the Miss Moviola scenario re-enacted over and over again. *Thanks but no thanks...*

But Ruth kept insisting, and finally she persuaded me to call him and set up an audition: She marched me into the bedroom, put the phone in my hand, and dialed his number. When he answered, I hemmed and hawed and finally blurted out that I'd heard he was looking for a vocalist. In his perverse way, he assured me he wasn't, and I got the feeling he was concerned that the nature of our relationship might make him less than objective about my merits as a singer. Fair enough; I understood that. I told him that I'd be willing to audition for him just like anyone else. After a bunch of palavering, he finally agreed that I could have an audition the following week when the band rehearsed.

On the day of the audition, I showed up early at the rehearsal. Frank and the band were jamming with an exotic-looking gent in flowing white robes and shaved head, playing an *extremely custom* fretted instrument that looked like an eight-stringed electric aluminum frying pan. He played it very well and it sounded quite groovy, as I recall. I don't know what he was doing there; I never saw him again.

Then Frank motioned me up on the stage with the band. As I stepped up onto the riser, I caught the sole of my shoe on the top step and nearly tripped. Frank grabbed my hand and pulled me up just in time. He wasn't in a good mood that day, and his whole body reflected his attitude. You had to give him high marks for honesty, if nothing else; if his head happened to be up his ass, he left it there without apology.

"Mistake number one," he commented nastily.

He handed me the libretto to "Hunchentoot," opened to the lyrics of a song called "Flambay." I asked if there was a lead sheet; he shook his head. *Great,* I thought, *I've got to learn this by ear in 15 seconds or less.*

Unfortunately for me, "Flambay" was in the key of C, with most of the melody falling in my upper register, which meant that if I tried to follow the original registration, at least half of the time I'd be screeching around in my 'break'. To avoid this, I had to sing the melody an octave lower, but because the song had been written for a higher voice, the timbre Frank wanted was therefore absent. Far worse, though, was the fact that I had nothing in common with the character of Drakma. Bette Midler would probably have beén a shoo-in for the role... Well, whatever my shortcomings, at least I've never been an actress. I was forced to treat the tune as if it were a guitar part, and approach it from a strictly melodic standpoint. At least the melody was nice — irregular and haunting.

I must have gotten carried away by the song, because suddenly it was over. I opened my eyes and looked to Frank for his reaction. Not good. His lips were tight, and he was looking down intently at his guitar. Something was eating him.

"How'd I do?" I asked.

"You were getting the intervals wrong," was all he said.

"Do I get the part?" I asked, half-seriously.

"No," he said flatly, and turned his back to me.

Figuring that he probably hadn't wanted to discuss business in front of the band, I called him that night and asked him to give me an objective evaluation of my performance and tell me why I hadn't passed the audition. I was surprised when he didn't comment on my singing, but instead launched into a speech about how if I'd been hired for the road band, I'd have had to be able to hang out with the other musicians. I think he might have hired me if I'd been anybody else, but he obviously didn't want a repeat of what had happened on the earlier tour.

Frank auditioned a vast quantity of singers for "Hunchentoot", but so many of the women trying out for Drakma's part expressed strong objections about the 'misogynism' of the material that he decided to scrap the whole project.

One day I met Ray Collins at the rehearsal facility. He had been one of the co-founders of the original Mothers, a bartender/vocalist Frank had salvaged from the netherworld of Inland Empire R & B bar bands back in the early '60s. His Irish whisky tenor crooning "Duke of Prunes," "America Drinks & Goes Home,""Oh No," and many another of Frank's more melodic compositions, was one of my most indelible adolescent memories. Evidently, though, his days of glory were behind him; when he had a little money, he stayed at the St. Moritz Hotel, a fleabag next to the rehearsal hall, and when he was broke (most of the time), he floated. Frank, I noticed, treated him quite indifferently, not paying much attention to him.

Ray had a band, of sorts, which rehearsed in Beverly Hills at the house of the bass player's father. I attended one of their rehearsals. It consisted of six cases of beer and four hours of the band members arguing about how to arrange Ray's song "Mr. Nixon, I Want Your Job" — one chord and two phrases of lyrics. Another night we stopped by the Whisky a Go Go in the heart of the swingin' Sunset Strip, to see some band Ray knew. It was quite a nostalgic evening; there were a number of people in attendance who had hung out with the Mothers, Vito, Carl Franzoni, and that whole 'freak' crowd on the Strip, and after the show, when everybody sat down on the wooden benches up in the back, the tall tales were flying. As I listened, I had the feeling that musty history was coming to life right before my eyes — until I remembered that 1965 was only nine years ago. Funny how some gray hair, a few missing teeth, and rapidly changing popular culture can make a not quite middle-aged bohemian seem like Rip van Winkle.

I let Ray, who was flat broke again, spend a couple of weeks on the sofa at my place so he wouldn't have to sleep on a park bench somewhere. While he was there, he got a windfall — a check from Frank Zappa Music, Inc. (BMI). The check was for $35.03 — total quarterly royalty residuals for all the songs he'd written or co-written on the early Mothers albums. (Later Frank would sue MGM/Verve Records for massive mishandling of the band's royalty proceeds over a period of more than a decade.) I cashed it for him, and he squandered the proceeds on Wonder Bread, Velveeta, Oscar Mayer bologna, Miracle Whip, and Coors.

Ray didn't look much different than he had in the '60s, but nobody seemed to recognize him, even people who should have. I knew a fey little lesbian singer/songwriter, an acquaintance of Frank's, who claimed to be a total early Mothers fanatic. One morning I happened to stop by her house on an errand, with Ray in tow. He chatted pleasantly with her for an hour, in the very same voice that had imprinted "Call Any Vegetable" on a budding generation of mutant minds. She hadn't the vaguest idea who she was talking to.

When I asked Frank why he was so indifferent to Ray's plight, he looked at me like I was a cretin and snorted, "*Too much acid.*" There had apparently been a fair amount of bad blood between them, off and on, since the old days. Ray told me some amusing stories about those bygone years, like the time Frank got into a donnybrook with a heckler when the Soul Giants were playing in a redneck sports bar in Pomona, and Ray had had to dive in and rescue him from the slaughter while there was still some of him left to save for musical posterity. A 135-pound, blues - guitar-playing Sicilian-American conceptualist is no match for a corn-fed Inland Empire football fan in a John Deere cap, regardless of how incensed the former might be about regarding slights on his masculinity. But there were tranquil moments as well — Ray recalled sitting around on the front porch one afternoon in Ontario with Frank and the first Mrs. Zappa, a bubbly blonde who was a teller at a local bank. The summer breeze was blowing the smog back toward Los Angeles, the bees were droning in the honeysuckle...And then who should come meandering up the garden path but a young, buxom redhead, who settled comfortably into a chair and began pleasantly explaining how Frank had recently met her in a Hollywood coffeehouse and told her if she'd come to the great Inland Empire, he'd make her the next big thing in low budget movies... Cut to a Cucamonga storefront that has been converted into a recording studio and living quarters, of sorts. Prominently displayed on the studio wall are the divorce papers Frank's now-ex-wife has served on him, and sharing the premises with the new bachelor is none other than Big Red, queen of the "Z" film and future star of that soon-to-be-a-regional-hit X-rated tape; Detective Willis of the San Berdoo vice squad can be glimpsed lurking on the periphery, about to pounce. There is no indoor plumbing to speak of. Idyllic.

Back in the early days of the Mothers, Ray had opined in a band meeting that what Frank needed to become a *real human being* was "to go to Big Sur and take acid with someone who believes in God." For some reason this suggestion was not followed up on.

Not long after Ray's grocery binge, Frank asked me to tell him that he wanted to use him as a backup vocalist on the new album he was recording, which turned out to be "Apostrophe'." I guess he didn't feel comfortable calling the front desk of the St. Moritz and leaving his old colleague a message.

I don't know what ultimately happened to Ray. For awhile I'd see him around town, walking down Sunset Boulevard, sometimes driving a cab. When my first book on Mark Twain was published, he got my number from Frank and called me to say he liked it. And then one day I suddenly realized I hadn't seen him or thought about him in years. But I still think "Oh No" and "America Drinks & Goes Home" are two of the greatest songs ever recorded.

In 1975 Frank worked briefly with Captain Beefheart (Don Van Vliet), who did a U.S. tour with him, singing and playing harmonica. Don was a phenomenal blues singer, an interesting poet, an erratic but intriguing painter and sculptor, and above all, an incredible conversationalist. He

RICK BURIAN

Me and Captain Beefheart

had been one of my (other) favorite people since 1970, when I'd met him, entirely coincidentally, through a distant acquaintance who had interviewed him for a magazine article. Over a period of a few days we sat talking around the clock while he drew in his sketchbook and I played the guitar. I'd also sat in with him and some of the members of his Magic Band, and Don had gone on to suggest that he should produce an album

127

One of Captain Beefheart's portraits of me

by me and a drummer friend of mine. A deal was struck, but a week before recording was supposed to start, he suddenly decided to move from the L.A. area to Ben Lomond in the Santa Cruz Mountains. I went up there to find out what was going on, wondering what sort of flake he was, only to discover that he had simply shifted gears and entirely forgotten about it. Turned out he was always doing things like that. I learned not to hold it against him. We stayed on good terms, and we usually got together to chew the rag when he visited southern California to visit his widowed mother in Lancaster.

Frank had been unaware of the nature of my relationship with Don until I ran into Don during a rehearsal and we went across the street to a coffee shop to chat. Evidently I'd stumbled into a very old and convoluted rivalry; when we came back after the break, Frank was glowering at me, bristling the way he had on tour when he thought I was being overly friendly with one of the guys in the band. It amazed me that his radar was still armed and pulling in things like that.

During the time he was rehearsing with Frank for the upcoming tour, Don was staying with his mother Sue in her trailer — uh, prefabricated home — in Lancaster. He apparently got bored one night watching TV, and called me at about two in the morning. The whole situation was made infinitely more complicated by the fact that I was newly married (to Lionel Rolfe, a fellow writer). Don, not knowing I was now a respectable (?) married woman, invited me to come out for a visit. (Logistics was never his forte.) I explained that I had a husband now, and politely asked if I could bring him along. Don griped and grumbled, but finally assented. We agreed to meet at the Denny's (ALWAYS OPEN) at the Sand Canyon offramp of the Antelope Valley Freeway. Back in the '50s he and Frank had whiled away the wee small hours at that selfsame Denny's; as Frank once observed, "There wasn't anything else to do in Lancaster." Some things never change. I personally felt rather honored to be part of this high desert intellectual tradition.

The three of us hit it off splendidly and spent ten hours, to the abject dismay of the management, drinking coffee (?) and chewing the rag. Don had his sketchbook at his elbow the whole time, doodling copiously; he showed us several sketches he had recently made of Frank with his guitar, which were easily the best drawings of Zappa I'd ever seen.

At daybreak, we walked out to the parking lot where Don's new Volvo sedan and our 1965 Citroen ID station wagon were parked side by side, the only vehicles in the enormous Denny's parking lot. Squinting into the dusty Antelope Valley sunrise, we gazed at the forest of bristling

Nike missile spikes on top of the nearest mountain peak. Suddenly, without a word, Don opened the trunk of the Volvo and extracted a pair of plaster-of-Paris wings with harness straps attached. "Frank gave these to me yesterday," he explained. They were the wings he had worn in *Captain Beefheart vs. the Grunt People,* the no-budget movie on which he and Frank had collaborated in Cucamonga in 1964.

Somehow word got back to Frank that I'd been out hobnobbing with Don in the desert. The next time I saw him, he gave me a peeved sort of look and razzed me about how I'd been *"blowing Van Vliet's harmonica."* I wondered just what deep, dark teenage tortures that flippant statement was hiding.

Captain Beefheart and me

RICK BURIAN

CHAPTER 12

Use a Typewriter, Go to Prison

I don't remember actually sitting down and deciding I never wanted to see Frank again. Our relationship had certainly changed over the years, and I no longer entertained any illusions that I would either be involved in playing his music, or that our personal situation would resume on its old scale, but even as the end drew near, I still hadn't reached the point where I felt that I'd be better off not having *anything* to do with him.

I'd known Frank for almost five years, and on *some* level I understood that there was a single fact which could not be overlooked, rationalized, or otherwise swept under the carpet: Nobody owned him, and nobody ever could. In a way, I was glad I wasn't married to him. His life was his work, and vice versa. He never socialized; when he was at home, as I'd seen, he crawled into the basement until such time as he needed to sleep, which he did for ten or twelve hours — then, back to the old workbench. Why, it was almost medieval. Then, after a few months of this creatively edifying but sociopathic *basement-hunkering*, it was Out on the Road, with all that *that* implied. Yessir — *this is your life, Frank Zappa.* In my more cynical moments I wondered how he'd wound up with two (later four) kids on that sort of schedule.

Still, even though I knew the truth, accepting it was another matter entirely. Late one afternoon I stopped by a rehearsal, my first in a long while. Frank seemed glad to see me, and afterward we sat on the stage talking. The band had packed up and gone home, and as we chatted about this and that, the crew was busy shutting off the lights and sound equipment. Finally the last technician called "Good night", rolled down the door, and locked it behind him, leaving us alone in the empty rehearsal hall with a single worklight glowing dimly overhead.

I began to be vaguely uneasy. Frank wasn't making any move to get going, which wasn't his usual order of business. I wondered if, or when, someone was supposed to pick him up. "Do you need a ride up the hill?" I asked. "Nope," he said, without elaboration. I noticed that his guitar case and briefcase were sitting next to his chair, ready to go.

At this point it had been quite a while since we'd had a physical relationship, but with my guard down a little, I was ashamed to realize I was still an open circuit for his peculiar electricity; just sitting there hearing his voice was enough to make me keyed up and a little dangerous. He gave me a sideways glance, and there was a hint of that old twinkle in his eyes. I shivered a little, although outside the temperature was close to eighty.

He didn't say anything further. There was a bathroom to the right of the stage, in the corner near the front entrance. It took maybe 15 seconds to get down off the stage riser, walk to the bathroom, and lock the door. I think he went first; at least I hope so.

I did stop seeing him not long after that, not because I wanted to, but because of, as they say, circumstances beyond my control.

I had been doing more freelance writing for magazines and newspapers, and almost making a living at it. It was amusing telling people that I'd gotten fed up with being a poverty stricken musician and had decided to go into writing for a living instead.

My livelihood put me in an awkward position with Frank. As he had become more and more well known, his mistrust of journalists had increased exponentially. Even though having the potential to write and sell articles on **Frank Zappa** was a lot like having money in the bank that I couldn't touch, I didn't want to do it, broke as I was. Nothing I had to say on the subject seemed important enough for me to contradict my indignant self-defense to Frank back in the Holiday Inn on West 57th Street — *"this stuff is private, and it's going to remain that way!"*

Then an editor I knew gave me an assignment to write a magazine piece; I can't even remember what the subject was anymore. I was supposed to get brief humorous quotes from people of my choice about whatever-it-was. Obliviously, not thinking about the ramifications, I called Frank, told him what I was writing, and asked if he'd like to comment on whatever-it-was. Maybe I was unconsciously trying to break loose from him. If so, I succeeded.

He was in a foul mood that night. Not only did he insult me for daring to think I had the right to call him up and ask him *a trivial and annoying question* for publication in an *idiotic article* in a *worthless magazine* , but he launched into a rant in which he accused me of *attempting to extort information out of him, put words in his mouth* , and somehow *subvert the American Way of free speech.*

All I could say was, "OK, Frank," and hang up. I sat there shaking my head and wondering, *"Why am I doing this to myself?"* It felt even worse than it should have, because I suspected I should never have done it in the first place.

The next day I wrote him a letter in which I told him I was sorry our friendship, or whatever it was, had to end this way, but he had made me feel worse than anyone had ever made me feel in my life before, and since I wouldn't be able to trust him after that, it was pointless to keep up the pretense. I said I guess he didn't care anymore, but he had been the most inspiring person I'd ever known, and that was why it hurt so much to see him diminish himself as well as me.

I sent the letter by registered mail. Somewhere deep down inside I hoped we would reconcile, but deeper yet, I knew things had changed too much for that to be possible. I also knew he wasn't likely to forgive me for what he would probably perceive as my treachery. I didn't expect him to write me back an answer. I wondered vaguely if he might call, but I wasn't surprised that he didn't.

In a week I got the return receipt back, signed. It was ironic but somehow absurdly appropriate that our relationship, which had begun with a letter from him to me, was now ending with a letter from me to him.

My time with Frank Zappa was clearly over. He was wrong; time wasn't a constant, it was a *one-shot deal* : horribly compressed and foreshortened. Ironically, the more time that went by without my seeing him, the more I realized how true that was.

Several months later I received a promotional copy of Frank's new album, "One Size Fits All." The cover featured a painting of the maroon sofa from the basement, floating in the heavens. On the back cover was an elaborate star map, full of in-jokes and private references to people Frank knew. I noticed that I was included, and I assumed that the artwork for the album had probably been done back before Frank and I went our separate ways, and he just hadn't bothered to change it.

I put the record on the turntable and gave it a spin. It was all familiar material, with the exception of a song called "Andy" on side two. That cut gave me a peculiar feeling the first time I played it -- its relentless rhythms made me a bit antsy. I went back and played it again while reading the lyrics, and I suddenly realized that the song was about me. The lyrics -- full of references to our relationship, sexual and emotional -- were Frank's answer to my letter. Well, I reasoned, if he could use his composition "RDNZL" to titillate me, then why couldn't he utilize *this* tune to castigate me? As fed up as I was with Frank, I couldn't help noticing that there was a bitter sadness in the song, a sense of loss and anger. It was truly ironic: neither of us had ever been able to communicate our true feelings to one another, but this was probably the closest Frank ever got to telling me what he actually felt. Unfortunately, the old unanswered question "Something...anything?", which had haunted our relationship right to the end, was likely to be the last word for us both.

CHAPTER 13

Goodnight, Boys and Girls

After our final rift, I had to teach myself not to think about Frank. It was a discipline, and for what seemed like an eternity, it required a superhuman effort; I hadn't realized just how much he had permeated my life and thinking until I had to make a clean break. I tried to be ruthlessly thorough — I threw away letters, tour itineraries, photos, anything with any sentimental value that might trigger a relapse. I even went so far as to unload my collection of albums, including the German copy of "Absolutely Free" Frank had brought back from a European tour for me, and refs and acetates for "The Grand Wazoo" and "Over-Nite Sensation."

Eventually, I kicked the habit. I no longer looked at situations the way he would have, or made little asides in his tone of voice (for a long while after my time with him I actually *sounded* like him — our voices and speech patterns were strangely similar to begin with, and when I was around him on a daily basis it didn't take me long to lose my vocal identity entirely. I wasn't the only one — practically everybody who worked for him sooner or later started imitating him). In short, I grew up, moved on, and left that whole phase of my life where it belonged — in the past. In the immortal words of Guitar Slim — "well, I done got over it".

It never occurred to me that all there had to be an outlet for all the intense emotions that had built up during my time with Frank. He had been such a powerful, all-pervasive influence on me that there wasn't a single area of my life he hadn't affected. You don't amputate a vast part of your soul without having an emotional hemorrhage. For me, the fall-out wouldn't occur until Frank's death some 15 years later, but that unfinished business would nearly finish me emotionally.

In 1985 Lionel and I were working for the B'nai B'rith Messenger, Los Angeles's oldest Jewish newspaper (*hey, a job's a job, right?*), and one day a very intense young lady showed up at the office. She turned out to be a writer for a heavy metal magazine, and she also claimed to be a good pal of Frank's. Frank had just testified before Congress about Tipper Gore and the Parents' Music Resource Committee's attempt to censor rock 'n' roll records with obligatory warning stickers, and this girl was apparently doing 'deep background' research work to help him fight the PMRC. She had dug up some rather incriminating xeroxes of position papers from a PMRC auxiliary group, stating that the Star of David was a Satanic symbol, and she figured the Messenger might be interested in an article showing that the PMRC's policies weren't just dangerous to headbangers and Joe Six-Pack, but to Jews as well.

Lionel has always been resoundingly indifferent to rock 'n' roll (in fact, Frank had liked Lionel better than Lionel liked him, which I found both amusing and a little sad), but he decided to publish the PMRC/*Menace to Judaism* article anyway. He also spoke to Frank by phone to get a few quotes for a sidebar. Frank was quite friendly, and he extended an informal invitation that could have been construed to mean, "Stop by and say hi sometime if you're in the neighborhood." I was glad that he didn't seem to have held a grudge, but at that point, the last time I'd been in the vicinity of Laurel Canyon and Mulholland had been more than ten years ago...

Around this time I saw Frank on CNN, testifying before Congress about the PMRC. He looked older, more crotchety and perverse than ever, and was dressed like an upscale *cucina nuovo* restauranteur: slick Armani suit and silk tie, sideburns starting to go gray, the old mad mane replaced by a short haircut, and his formerly dark, square goatee now speckled with silver and neatly manicured. However, when he started fulminating against the "Washington Wives," I stood solemnly in front of the tube and gave him the Sicilian fist-up *Va' Fanculo* salute. The world was such an absurd place, and America the capital of all absurdity; in a cosmos based on poetic irrationality, he would have been President for Life, and the lyrics to our National Anthem would have been unprintable. He wouldn't have had to wear that monkey suit anymore, either — although, knowing how contrary Citizen Honker could be, he probably *liked* it.

In 1990 I was having dinner with a couple of friends, and they happened to mention that they'd heard Frank had been diagnosed with prostate cancer. This news came as a shock to me, but it felt a bit remote, like I was hearing about a distant acquaintance or a relative I hadn't seen in years. Very few of my friends, even the closest ones, knew much

© 1995 PHIL STERN

about my relationship with Frank; it was so far back in my past that it wasn't something I thought about anymore.

During the next three years, I kept hearing reports about Frank's health. Sometime in 1992, my friend Phil Stern, a photographer I've known for a long time, was called to do a photo shoot at Raleigh Studios in Hollywood. A commercial was being filmed for an ecologically-minded utility company, and the spokesman they had selected was none other than Frank Zappa, that staunch friend of the environment. Phil's a tough cookie; sometimes he gives the impression he never left Anzio beach-head (he was a member of the Darby's Rangers unit during World War II, and was famous for the countless photos he sent to Life magazine from the European front), and he's been around Hollywood long enough not to be impressed by anyone or anything. A lifelong jazz fan, — he's known for his trademark shots of Billie Holliday, Louis Armstrong, Joe Turner, and Ella Fitzgerald, among numerous others — Phil didn't know anything about Frank Zappa, and was entirely prepared to leave it that way, but during a break in the shooting, Frank walked right up to him, put his hand out, and observed: "You're the only guy on this set who knows what the fuck he's doing." Then he proceeded to compliment Phil on some of his photographs, with which he seemed to be familiar. Phil, needless to say, was charmed.

When I looked at the photos of Frank which Phil took that day, they spoke eloquently of how his illness had taken its toll; his shoulder-length, formerly jet-black hair was more than half silver, and his face was crossed by delicate lines. His old earthiness was still apparent, but now it seemed tempered with a depth and complexity reminiscent of a portrait of a Renaissance philosopher: Dr. Zurkon had merged into Fulcanelli.

Near the end of 1992, I read in the paper that Frank hadn't been able to attend a four-day tribute concert of his music in New York on account of his failing health. At the event his daughter Moon had read a prepared statement to the press admitting that he had prostate cancer. Finally, on December 5, 1993, a friend called to say she'd been listening to Howard Stern's radio show, and Stern had announced that Frank had died the day before. He hadn't quite made it to his fifty-third birthday, which would have been on the 21st.

At first I couldn't believe Frank was...dead. Maybe, like Mark Twain, his demise had been greatly exaggerated. How could this stalwart crank, who had survived false imprisonment, near-fatal assault and battery, and more than 25 years of 'mystery meals' in Holiday Inns around the globe, have been tripped up in the end by a mutinous gaggle of his own cells?

The pain of his loss was so intense it was physical. Every confused, contradictory, unresolved emotion I'd ever felt toward him came welling up in me, until I felt I would choke to death. But the good things

I remembered about Frank were infinitely more painful — the teasing warmth of his voice, the strange weather in his eyes, the way he'd looked that afternoon conducting "RDNZL" for an audience of one...I couldn't bear to lose him twice like this.

One bright, windy morning a couple of days later, I got on the freeway and drove sixty miles into the Mojave Desert, to Palmdale. Frank had spent his high school days a few miles farther north in Lancaster. I turned off Pearblossom Highway onto a dirt road, where there were no houses, and got out of the car. For half an hour or maybe longer, I stood there screaming until I was hoarse. It didn't make me feel any better, but I had lost all sense of control. I couldn't stop myself.

Eventually I came to the realization that these emotions were primal enough to kill me, and I fumbled to find a constructive outlet for them. Not knowing what else to do, I began hesitantly writing about Frank

©1995 PHIL STERN

Zappa the way I remembered him, as if that could somehow make him re-corporate. For me he'd often been as much an idea as a flesh-and-blood human being; maybe I could make him exist again through the written word, just as, conversely, his music had always seemed so physical to me.

Here, some eight months later, is the result of my experiment. I don't know if I have managed to capture that elusive "when", but if I have brought back to life the Frank Zappa I knew, fought with, learned from, and loved — and recaptured my time with him — then maybe Time is really just a construct after all.

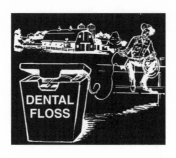

Selected Discography and Notes

atching Frank work in the studio could be painful; he'd start with a live recording that was breathtaking, then he'd begin to pick it apart and piddle with it and over-dub this and take out that, and before you knew it, he wound up with a result that was considerably less than the sum of its parts. Details were always his Achilles' heel. (The "Over-Nite Sensation" and "Apostrophe'" albums are prime examples of this.) And yet (*sez I*), he *still* made some of the greatest records of all time, *when* he was able to stay out of his own way. In the following discography I have listed several listening suggestions for each chapter, with the more option-al choices marked with an asterisk (*). All titles in this discography are in print on CD as of this writing, unless otherwise indicated.

Chapter 1: Meet Mr. Honker

FREAK OUT!
"You're Probably Wondering Why I'm Here": This song really stuck with me for some reason, even though at the time the album was released (1966) I was eleven years old and had no idea about the Sunset Strip scene being satirized in the song. It's still a great universally scathing condem-nation of diehard hipsterism, even if some of the references are dated.

"Trouble Comin' Every Day": Frank's view of the Watts riots of 1965 is worth listening to today. If the 1965 references were updated slightly, the entire song could be about the Los Angeles riots of 1992. As he did with much of his material, he re-arranged and re-recorded this number more than once, but I still prefer the original version for its urban electric blues sound. When Frank says "Blow your harmonica, son" near the end, it's positively surreal.

* **"Help, I'm a Rock"**: Here's the mumbling, fulminating, and percussion. Frank got better at this sort of thing as he went on, but it still has some funny moments, especially if you imagine scowling, eleven-year-old me in front of my record player, listening to this cut with the volume cranked and my bedroom door open. I'm sure Frank wrote "Help, I'm a Rock" with people like my mother in mind; he had a similar experience with his own mother the first time he ever listened to Varèse's *Ionisation* on the family phonograph.

HOT RATS

Play the whole thing, and turn it all the way up. I still think "Hot Rats" is the best thing Frank ever recorded for several reasons, the most important being that he wasn't working with an existing band; this was strictly a studio project, which enabled him to start with a blank canvas and create a sort of virtual audio reality. The droll, warm, pseudo-symphonic humor of **"Peaches en Regalia"** is a perfect musical reflection of a mood I saw Frank exhibit more than once, but which he never came close to capturing on any of his other recordings. (There's a little of that same feeling in spots on the much later *MAKE A JAZZ NOISE HERE* CD, but enough of that.) **"It Must Be a Camel"** has breathtaking, *sui generis* harmonies and sections where the lead instruments (sax, electric violin, and guitar) are braided together so tightly that you literally can't tell which is which. "Hot Rats" changed the way I thought about music forever, and it might very well do the same for you, if you've never heard it before. (If any of this fascinates you, try to get hold of the old vinyl version and listen to that as well; it's considerably different than the CD, which was digitally 'refurbished' and has chunks edited out of each selection; the CD has also been entirely re-mixed, not always to its benefit.)

* **Captain Beefheart and His Magic Band: *TROUT MASK REPLICA***
Frank produced this record by his old high school buddy Don Van Vliet in 1969. When I met Don in late 1970, he was going through one of his periodic anti-Zappa phases (something he did with fair regularity). He'd

144

spend hours chain-smoking evil-smelling Balkan Sobranie cigarettes, listening to "Trout Mask" over and over again, and bitching about the production, the art direction, the color of the label, etc., etc., etc. I found it really entertaining to watch him sitting there, choking in the Sobranie fog, shaking his fist at the stereo, and calling Frank highly original names — especially since "Trout Mask" is, in my humble opinion, not only Beefheart's finest hour, but one of the best records ever made in *any* genre. My favorite selection on "Trout Mask" is **"The Blimp"**, which consists of a riff borrowed from the Mothers' cut "Didja Get Any Onya" (that section of the track wasn't originally included on the "Weasels Ripped My Flesh" album, but it was restored on the CD release more than 20 years later). Over this riff Don's cousin Victor Haydon, who's calling in to the studio from a phone booth, hysterically recites lyrics like, *"It's the big hit! It's the blimp, Frank! It's the blimp!"* and *"Tits, tits! The blimp, the blimp!"* There are a lot of other outstanding songs on "Trout Mask" (like **"Moonlight On Vermont"** and **"Pachuco Cadaver"**), but "The Blimp" is the only one where the artist refers so humorously to the producer's, er, deficiencies, real or imagined... (Don's monicker 'Captain Beefheart', incidentally, was an invention of Frank's, and derived from the fact that Don's uncle, back in the old days in Lancaster, had been in the habit of exposing himself to Don's girlfriend, all the while mumbling superlatives about his member: "Ah— looks like a fine *beef heart* ...")

For more on Zappa and Beefheart, see notes to *BONGO FURY* , below.

Chapter 2: The Short Hello

YOU CAN'T DO THAT ON STAGE ANYMORE, Volume I
"Once Upon a Time" and **"Sofa # 1"** are live recordings of the first two 'movements' of the "German material." They were recorded at the disastrous Rainbow Theatre concert in London at which Frank met his Waterloo by being shoved into the orchestra pit. Unfortunately this show came a week after the fire at the Montreux Casino which destroyed all of the band's equipment. The group was limping by with makeshift gear after a hastily retooling, so the instrumentation is somewhat austere. Imagine, if you will, the addition of a concertina, a clarinet, and (ahem), some extra vocal power from yours truly, and you'll get the true flavor of this fine Zappa opus.

Here are some of the compositions with which I was confronted during my initial runthrough with Frank:

145

* **"Uncle Meat/Dog Breath"** (which appears in various permutations on several different recordings, but the closest, appropriately enough, is on the *UNCLE MEAT* CD (worth a listen for other reasons; it's one of Frank's best). There is no 'live' recording on any of Frank's CD's which exactly replicates the version I played, and it was not part of the repertoire of that particular touring band).

Selections (at random) from **"Billy the Mountain"** , which appears in its entirety on *PLAYGROUND PSYCHOTICS* , of which more below.

A medley of **"Status Back Baby"**, **"Concentration Moon"**, and **"Mom & Dad"**. These were all earlier compositions, re-arranged and glued together with shtick and dialogue, as well as quotes from Stravinsky (the ominous *Agon* fanfare, *Petrouchka* , and *The Rite of Spring*). The sequence is featured on *PLAYGROUND PSYCHOTICS* .

* **"Mystery Roach"** , from the *200 MOTELS* soundtrack (not available on CD as of this writing).

Chapter 5: For *This* I Learned to Play Stravinsky??!

Examples of Frank's guitar playing could cover an entire discography by themselves. Here are a few suggestions:

* **"The Village Inn"**, **"Power Trio Segment from 'The Saints 'N' Sinners'"**, **"Speed Freak Boogie"**, and **"The Original Mothers at the Broadside (Pomona)"** from *THE OLD MASTERS, Box 1* (from the 'Mystery Disc'). An expensive investment, featured on the final disc of a seven-disc boxed set, released only on vinyl — but highly indicative of Frank's early guitar style, as he never released any other examples of his pre-Mothers playing. Also includes some early tracks ('63-'64) with Captain Beefheart. Just how hardcore *are* you, anyway?

On **"Status Back Baby"** on the *PLAYGROUND PSYCHOTICS* CD, Frank pulls off a flawless (well, almost) version of the *Agon/Petrouchka* stunt. (It *was* recorded at the end of the tour.) Also on *PLAYGROUND PSYCHOTICS* , there's a brief example of what he sounded like on a good night: **"Brixton Still Life"**. Over an essentially nondescript one-chord vamp, he goes from space-jazz, suspended chords to kick-ass funk to convoluted lines — a fine projection of numerous attitudes in three minutes.

There are two interesting, somewhat uncharacteristic semi-acoustic inter-ludes on *WEASELS RIPPED MY FLESH* : **"Toads of the Short Forest"** and **"Dwarf Nebula Processional March"**. "Toads of the Short Forest" was a pre-Mothers composition, dating back to the Studio Z era ('63-'64); Frank plays the 'head' a little stiffly, but the tune is one of the most effective guitar pieces I've ever heard by anybody. "Dwarf Nebula Processional March" features the novelty of Frank playing what sounds like a *gut-string guitar* . It also has a fascinating, graceful-but-obsessive little melody which breaks every harmony-book resolution rule but is steadfastly, strangely beautiful. Frank seemed to be drawn to medieval *anything* ; this piece could be called *neo-medieval* . Finally, if you're a hardcore Zappa listener, there's a truly one-of-a-kind moment in **"Get A Little"**: the only *obvious guitar clinker* Frank ever released on a recording. A little past the middle section of the solo, his hand inad-vertently slips, resulting in six passing tones that aren't part of the scale. Non-musicians — most listeners, actually — probably wouldn't even notice. It's a safe bet Frank did, however.

* **"Transylvania Boogie"**, from *CHUNGA'S REVENGE* , is worth a lis-ten if you want a sterling example of Frank's guitar strengths and weak-nesses side-by-side. He plays the Hungarian minor introduction as though he's having his wisdom teeth pulled without Novocaine; each note in the scale is more painfully wrought than the one before it. But when the solo gets rolling and he's on more comfortable terrain, he grabs hold of that same scale and teaches it a trick or two. In another mood entirely is * **"Twenty Small Cigars"** (which started life back in the Studio Z days as an insipid vocal that began, "If you say goodbye/I know that I will surely die."). It's one of the prettiest guitar melodies that Frank, or anybody, ever wrote.

"The Grand Wazoo", from the CD of the same name, kicks off with a striking, highly characteristic minor-eleventh opening chordal passage that still makes the hair on the back of my neck stand up. Those dense har-monies against a shuffle rhythm, tossed off with real authority, but sound-ing like the most casual of afterthoughts — that, folks, could only be Frank Zappa. (For more on *THE GRAND WAZOO* CD, see below.)

"Zoot Allures", from the eponymous CD, is another of Frank's pieces that takes modern guitar composition into the fifth dimension. This is as about as close as you can get to whatever it was that made Frank, and his music, so powerful, unsettling, and exhilarating.

Finally, one of Frank's most effective and exciting guitar solos, live or canned, is captured on the *MOTHERS/AHEAD OF THEIR TIME?* CD during **"The Orange County Lumber Truck"**. (This is the complete version of the song, which also appears in truncated form on *WEASELS RIPPED MY FLESH*.) Frank was always fond of downgrading the musicianship of the 'original' Mothers, but the spontaneous kick of hearing the entire band becoming audibly excited by Frank's solo and responding with ever-more-fevered playing, could have served as an object lesson for some of his later, more technically advanced but emotionally withdrawn, groups.

The * *SHUT UP ' N' PLAY YER GUITAR* and * *GUITAR* sets, while they may be fascinating to Zappa completists and fanatics (and/or rock guitar players), have an awful lot of the same thing — long guitar solos over fairly simple chordal backdrops. It should be kept in mind that during most of Frank's live performances (with the exception of a few tours in the late '70s and early '80s), the focus was on the compositions and arrangements rather than his guitar. In the 1971 band, as an example, he averaged five or six solos per show, none of them more than one or two minutes long. He really didn't need more time than that to drive home his point; with Frank, as with most things, brevity was the soul of wit. It's my suspicion that he began emphasizing long guitar solos in the late '70s because he hoped to attract a younger, primarily rock-oriented, audience as his older listeners began drifting away. He was a fine rock guitarist, but I think he was even better at other things — like composing, arranging, and bandleading. If you want to get into the minutiae of that particular aspect of his work, by all means don't let me stop you; but to me these collections come dangerously close to monotony — not a quality I'd otherwise associate with Frank Zappa.

Note : If you think some of the situations described in this chapter are science fiction, a listen to the earlier-mentioned *PLAYGROUND PSYCHOTICS* should convince you otherwise. This two-CD set, assembled by Frank in 1992, chronicles the approximate time span I'm describing (although it mostly covers the six months before I joined the tour, and then skips to the tail end, the Rainbow Theater show). Masterfully edited, it consists of 'field' recordings of band members in everyday road situations, interspersed with music from the shows. A rare anthropological artifact, and full of (sometimes painful) laughs.

Chapter 7: My Continuing Education

* "Igor's Boogie", on *BURNT WEENY SANDWICH* , may or may not have been arranged by my junior college Composition teacher, but it *does* sound Stravinskyesque. My composition "Opus One", mentioned in this chapter, was based on the opening piano theme to * **"Little House That I Used to Live In"** , also on *BURNT WEENY SANDWICH* .

Chapter 9: Home, Home and Deranged

Frank made a fine recording of **"RDNZL"** during the series of sessions in which he recorded parts of "Over-Nite Sensation" in late 1972. Because the band he had then was considerably smaller, the instrumentation was accordingly reduced from the original Grand Wazoo version, but there was certainly no loss of effect. When he went to mix the song, however, Frank detected the presence of *intrusive audio crud* which had somehow crept onto the tape. He evidently felt it made that version of **"RDNZL"** unreleasable. A similar 'live' version of **"RDNZL"** by that same (1972-74) band appears on *YOU CAN'T DO THAT ON STAGE ANYMORE, Vol. 2: The Helsinki Concert* . Although two other versions appear on the original *SLEEP DIRT* release and *YOU CAN'T DO THAT ON STAGE ANYMORE, Vol. 5* , respectively, Frank unfortunately never released a recording of **"RDNZL"** by the original Grand Wazoo line-up. See below.

THE GRAND WAZOO

This recording doesn't even come close to capturing the grandeur of the Wazoo, but it's still worth a listen. The title track (also known as **"The Grand Wazoo"**) has some good guitar playing on it; the *"rum-pum-pum"* wordless vocal on **"Cletus Awreetus-Awritus"** has been described by one listener as sounding like *"the high school band conductor singing the parts to the musicians".* (Said listener may have been closer to the truth than he realized.) There's more good guitar playing on **"Blessed Relief"**. The liner note story about Cletus Awreetus-Awritus, the funky emperor, and his valiant stand against the Mediocrites of Pedestrium, is a little like sitting around drinking cognac with Frank in a jovial mood and listening to him expound on his view of ancient history. Still, I'll bet a verbatim 'live' recording of the Wazoo's Hollywood Bowl concert (which included "RDNZL") on September 10, 1972 would have been the first record ever to win simultaneous Grammy awards in the Classical, Jazz, and Sarrusophone Solo categories...I'll bet...

Chapter 10: Statement of Earnings

OVER-NITE SENSATION
Many of the tracks for this CD and *APOSTROPHE'* were recorded during the same period; in fact, both albums are combined on the same CD release, although *OVER-NITE SENSATION* was released nearly a year before *APOSTROPHE'*. On the back cover of the vinyl version of *APOSTROPHE'* is the attribution "Produced, arranged and struggled with [by] Frank Zappa." Having witnessed these tracks being recorded, I can attest to the struggle. In the end, the music may have gotten away from him. One of the musicians described *OVER-NITE SENSATION* as being "like looking at the band through the wrong end of a telescope." Most of the female vocals are by Mrs. Ex-Big R&B Singer (whose identity should be apparent to most people, although her name isn't listed anywhere. Well, she's in good company — neither is mine). **"Fifty-Fifty"** features the dipsomaniacal vocal and George Duke's big organ solo described in this chapter. **"Dirty Love"** has Mrs. EBRBS's gospel-chorus-in-heat backup vocal and a 'live'-sounding guitar solo that required something in the vicinity of 24 takes. **"Montana"**, is, in my estimation, the most successful song on the CD, with its low-rent-Copland intro and absurd premise (*moving to Montana to raise dental floss*).

Chapter 11: No Commercial Potential

The song **"Flambay"** appears on the *SLEEP DIRT* CD.

Ray Collins was the lead vocalist on the *FREAK OUT! , ABSOLUTE-LY FREE* , and *CRUISING WITH RUBEN AND THE JETS* albums, as well as parts of *UNCLE MEAT*. His vocal on **"Oh No"** is featured on *WEASELS RIPPED MY FLESH* .

BONGO FURY
The *BONGO FURY* CD is the only commercially available recording (as opposed to various bootlegs) of a collaboration between Frank Zappa and Captain Beefheart (with the exception of the **"Willie the Pimp"** track on *HOT RATS* and the early stuff on the last record of the *OLD MASTERS* ,**Vol. I** boxed set). It's basically a 'live' recording, with some overdubs, and as such it has a rather 'unfinished' quality, but its premise is interesting. *BONGO FURY* chronicles Frank and Don's relationship — more or

less. **"Debra Kadabra"** is full of references to Don's adolescent fascination with cosmetics (his mother was an Avon Lady), and the no-budget monster movies Frank and Don used to watch (e.g., *Brainiac*, a low-tech Mexican groaner — the braying brass lick in the background was the movie's *actual leitmotif* for its guy-in-the-rubber-suit monster: "Make me grow Brainiac fingers, *but with more hair!"*) **"Cucamonga"** is straight autobiography, a semi-nostalgic description of the Studio Z days. So, to a certain extent, is **"Advance Romance"**. Don describes his surreal youth in **"Sam With the Showing Scalp Flat Top"**. Finally, Frank paints a characteristic scene from his *adult life* in **"Carolina Hardcore Ecstasy"**.

Note: For an interesting example of how Zappa and Beefheart influenced each other's music, compare Don's first single, * **"Diddy Wah Diddy"** (originally released on A&M Records in 1965, available on a 1984 A&M Records vinyl-only reissue, *CAPTAIN BEEFHEART: THE LEGENDARY A&M SESSIONS*) and Frank's 1966 single, * **"Why Don't You Do Me Right"**, now on the *ABSOLUTELY FREE* CD. They share the same growling vocal, fuzztone guitar, and harpsichord fills — and both records are based on the same menacing blues riff, copped from "Smokestack Lightnin'".

Chapter 12: Use a Typewriter, Go To Prison

The song **"Andy"** , in which Frank, evidently furious with me over our final 'disagreement', asks the burning question "Is there anything good inside of you? If there is, I really wanna know", appears on the *ONE SIZE FITS ALL* CD. If you're curious, my *other* (specific) appearance in Frank's catalogue is in **"Muffin Man"**, on *BONGO FURY* , in which he fulminates about my (largely imagined) relationship with Ray Collins (*AKA* the "Muffin Man", which is what Collins was called during the Garrick Theater days). ("Girl, you thought he was a man, but he was a muffin...You hung around 'til you found that he didn't know nothin.'")

THE YELLOW SHARK
Frank's last live (and first posthumous) recording. Faced with declining audiences at his rock shows, coupled with political difficulties in Europe that made touring abroad unfeasible, he spent the last ten or so years of his life composing on the Synclavier (a sophisticated digital composition and playback system) and, on occasion, working with 'classical' ensembles in presenting live and/or recorded concerts of his orchestral works.

This program incorporates various edits of live performances, a fact which is sometimes noticeable but rarely intrusive. Although *THE YELLOW SHARK* is marred by cloyingly worshipful, even servile annotation, the music — performed by the German-based Ensemble Modern — speaks pretty loudly for itself. Highlights include **"The Girl in the Magnesium Dress"** (an updated version of a piece earlier recorded by Pierre Boulez conducting the Ensemble Intercontemporain), a densely polyphonic work with more than a nod to the player piano compositions of Conlon Nancarrow, and **"G-Spot Tornado"** (previously recorded on the Synclavier on the *JAZZ FROM HELL* CD), which, especially in this orchestral incarnation, is one of the most riveting, rhythm-dominated, inexorable things Frank ever wrote. It's absurdly appropriate that the final composition on the last recording made before his death is a rousing, humorous paean to sex. That's probably as it should be. In a more sobering vein, evidence that Frank was becoming increasingly able to communicate his own emotional responses to larger issues is inherent in **"Time's Beach III"**, an elegiac movement from a larger work.

Debate on the topic of *Frank Zappa as Serious Composer* is pointless. That there is a degree of presumption in his orchestral works is undeniable; but even the staunchest Zappa detractor has to admit that some of his endeavors in this area are entirely successful on their own terms. For what it's worth, I have always felt that Frank's biggest weakness was also his greatest strength — his lack of formal training. His sneering at 'the academy' always seemed to have a tinge of wistfulness in it, as though he might as well sneer, since 'they' were never going to accept him anyway. His who-gives-a-fuck iconoclasm relegated him to the position of outcast and joker, and at the same time probably caused him to be victimized by his own penchant for detail rather than developing a more expansive philosophy, musical and otherwise (which was tragic, considering the breadth of his intellect). On the other hand, the absence of academic protocols and formalistic straitjacketing in his thinking was precisely what enabled him to formulate his own musical universe. Listening to *THE YELLOW SHARK,* I am saddened by the fact that Frank's life and output were cut short just when his work was showing so many signs of enlarging into something with much more emotional depth. (As this book went to press, his posthumous work "Civilization: Phaze III" was about to be released, but I hadn't yet heard it and could not pass judgment.) Had he lived and worked for a few more decades, he might have created music as monumental in its own way as Bartok's; he certainly had the potential. But the enormous body of work he left behind contains so many high points that the whole issue of what he *could* have accomplished is just as pointless as whether or not he should be considered a 'serious' composer. *He* took it seriously, and the music reflects that fact. Whatever the verdict of posterity (which has certainly never been known for a fine degree of discernment), Frank Zappa's music both defined and spoke for a generation during a critical period in human history. I am convinced it will continue to speak for future generations...if anyone is still around to listen.

Set in Italian Old Style with LoType headlines. 3,000 copies on acid-free paper were printed at McNaughton and Gunn lithographers, Saline, Michigan.